ADVANCE PRAISE FOR
CRUISE SHIP BLUES

The cruise line industry has a $500 million annual
advertising budget. The environment, workers
and customers of the industry have Ross Klein.
It's a more even contest than you might imagine.

— Robert Gibson, *Alternatives Journal*

Cruise Ship Blues is a mine of information about
what's changed, what hasn't, and what should change
in the cruise industry. No cruise charm, no dull travel
destination talk, no self-serving claims of corporate
responsibility — just sobering, informative, often
entertaining, first-person accounting, meticulously
researched. Sure to become an indispensable primer for
anyone considering a cruise vacation, and a must-read
for all those who endeavor to preserve the ocean realm.

— Coralie Breen, CEO/President, Oceans Blue Foundation

Come aboard the first in-depth examination of the
international cruise industry, and find out why advocates
for social justice, fair labor practices, equitable tax laws,
environmental protection, and competent medical care
have started paying attention to the ship "on the other
side of the curtain." Klein's below-deck tour scuttles the
"Love Boat" myth and exposes the fragile foundation
supporting a multi-billion dollar industry...

— Gershon Cohen, Ph.D., Project Director, Campaign to
Safeguard America's Waters, Earth Island Institute

For anyone who's ever been seduced by the cruise industry's slick ads, Ross Klein's fascinating exposé will make you think twice before booking your next voyage. The industry's dirty, dangerous and deceptive practices are more reminiscent of the Exxon Valdez than the "Love Boat," replete with scandalous tales of toxic pollution and bungled cover-ups, utter disdain for passenger health or safety, and above all, lurid accounts of greed trumping human and environmental welfare. This book causes outrage.

— Russell Long, Ph.D., former America's Cup Skipper, Executive Director, Bluewater Network

Behind all the hype and glitz of luxury cruising, there is a real story, told here by Ross Klein, whose expertise is founded on the personal experience of thirty cruises. Here "the underside of the industry is brought into daylight." Klein's readable and authoritative volume may not dim your enthusiasm for cruising, but it will open your eyes to a very troubling corporate culture that abuses both customers and workers, and threatens the environment; and it may save you some money. Forewarned is fore-armed.

— Paul Chapman, author of *Trouble on Board, the Plight of International Seafarers*

Cruise Ship Blues ...is well written and full of hard to get information for anyone — cruise lovers included. It shows how millions of relatively privileged individuals engage — mostly unreflected — in socially and ecologically unsustainable recreational behavior. A sustainable future would call for "soft tourism," implying that the wasteful, environmentally and socially damaging cruise industry be downsized...

— Isidor Wallimann, co-editor of *On the Edge of Scarcity: Environment, Resources, Population, Sustainability, and Conflict*

CRUISE SHIP
BLUES

THE UNDERSIDE
OF THE CRUISE
INDUSTRY

ROSS A. KLEIN

NEW SOCIETY PUBLISHERS

Cataloguing in Publication Data:
A catalog record for this publication is available from the National Library of Canada.

Cover design by Diane McIntosh. Larry Mulvehill, © Corbis Images.

Printed in Canada by Friesens.
Second Printing.

Paperback ISBN: 0-86571-462-2

To order directly from the publishers, please add $4.50 shipping to the price of the first copy, and $1.00 for each additional copy (plus GST in Canada). Send check or money order to:

New Society Publishers
P.O. Box 189, Gabriola Island, BC V0R 1X0, Canada
1-800-567-6772

New Society Publishers' mission is to publish books that contribute in fundamental ways to building an ecologically sustainable and just society, and to do so with the least possible impact on the environment, in a manner that models this vision. We are committed to doing this not just through education, but through action. We are acting on our commitment to the world's remaining ancient forests by phasing out our paper supply from ancient forests worldwide. This book is one step towards ending global deforestation and climate change. It is printed on acid-free paper that is **100% old growth forest-free** (100% post-consumer recycled), processed chlorine free, and printed with vegetable based, low VOC inks. For further information, or to browse our full list of books and purchase securely, visit our website at: www.newsociety.com

New Society Publishers   www.newsociety.com

TABLE OF CONTENTS

THE INAUGURAL SAIL:
AN INTRODUCTION TO THE
CRUISE INDUSTRY

SAILING THE SEAS ONBOARD A CRUISE SHIP, the days filled with luxury and pampering, perfect weather, glorious food, and impeccable service ... it's a dream vacation. What could be better than lounging on the deck of a floating resort, soaking up the sun, indulging in whatever fits your mood?

That image is what sells cruises. But do the people sitting in the sun, sipping those margaritas, realize the environmental and social cost of this indulgence? Are those passengers aware of the environmental practices of the cruise industry, of the lifestyle of the servers and staff aboard the ship, of the risks to safety and security that are part of everyday life on a cruise ship? The answer, unfortunately, is: likely not.

Most people who go on a cruise put anything that interferes with their vacation out of their mind. They are unconcerned about the pollution left in the ship's wake, or about employees working 16 hours a day, 7 days a week, for 10 to 12 months straight, at incomes below minimum wage. Nor do they give a thought to the risk of illness from food or injury from an accident. This is the part of the cruise experience that's left out of the brochures. It's not part of a cruise passenger's reality, but trust me, it exists.

IS THE CRUISE INDUSTRY SUSTAINABLE?

Cruise Ship Blues: The Underside of the Cruise Industry is guided by a simple question: is the cruise industry sustainable? The answer to this question has many parts. For example, is the industry environmentally sustainable? In other words, does the cruise industry treat the environment in such a way that leaves it undamaged? As well,

1

the facts behind the hidden lifestyle of shipboard workers and the cruise industry's economic record cast doubt on whether the industry is socially and morally sustainable. The answers to these questions, for many of us, are not encouraging. The fact is that the cruise industry has historically shown a disregard for the environment, for the welfare of its workers, and even for the well-being of its paying passengers. That is the focus of this book.

AN INDUSTRY OVERVIEW

Cruise ship vacations are the fastest growing segment of leisure travel. Since 1970 the number of people taking a cruise has increased by more than 1,000 percent. In North America the increase has been fivefold — from 1.4 million to almost 7 million passengers — over the 20-year period from 1980 to 2000. Worldwide, more than 12 million passengers boarded cruise ships in the year 2000.[1]

This growth pattern is expected to continue. Passenger capacity will increase by almost 50 percent from 2001 to 2005, between 8 and 15 percent annually. In February 2002 the cruise industry had on order 36 ships with more than 71,000 berths at a cost of $12.5 billion.* By the end of 2002, 12 new ships will have been introduced with accommodations for more than 20,000 additional passengers. In 2003 14 more ships will be added, with berths for another 30,000 passengers. Expect a further 10 new ships with accommodations for over 25,000 more passengers in 2004.[2]

Between 2000 and 2006, the industry will have increased its capacity by more than 100,000 beds. To put the scale of this growth into vivid perspective, consider that in 1981 the North American segment of the industry accommodated approximately 41,000 passengers. By 2006 that number is expected to exceed 260,000, according to the Cruise Line International Association (CLIA). Actual numbers are likely much higher since these figures are based on two people per room; many rooms can accommodate three or four passengers.

EXPANSION AND CONSOLIDATION

While the cruise industry's capacity is increasing, the number of companies in the marketplace is shrinking. There are two reasons for this.

---

*All sums of money are in US dollars.

Bankruptcies

The cruise industry's expansion would be even greater if it were not for seven cruise companies having ceased operations in 2000 and 2001. In 2000 Premier Cruises, Commodore Cruise Line (including its premium Crown Cruise Line), Cape Canaveral Cruise Line, and the World Cruise Company all filed for bankruptcy, eliminating more than 7,000 berths.

Both Marine Expeditions and Renaissance Cruises left passengers stranded when the companies unexpectedly filed for bankruptcy in 2001. The planned shutdown of American Classic Voyages in September 2001 left few passengers stranded, but it took three cruise lines out of the water: America Hawaii Cruises, Delta Coastal Voyages, and United States Line. That resulted in 9,000 fewer available berths.

The cruise line bankruptcies had grave consequences for consumers. Many people lost money paid as deposits; some lost their entire fare. Passenger refund claims totaled more than $110 million against Renaissance Cruises alone.

Surprisingly, the failure of American Classic Voyages also left thousands of consumers high and dry. Many people had assumed that, like other carriers operating from US ports, American Classic Voyages had posted a $15-million bond as required by the US government's Federal Maritime Commission. But after the company ceased operations, it came to light that because it had operated ships flagged in the USA, American Classic Voyages had been allowed to self-insure. As a result there was no bond and consumers were left with little recourse for refunds.

Takeovers and Mergers

Even greater than the impact of bankruptcies on the cruise industry landscape is the effect of takeovers and mergers. Consolidation of the industry began in the late 1980s and continues today. Carnival Corporation, the parent company of Carnival Cruise Lines, was the first to begin buying other cruise lines. The company was established in 1972 with a single ship that accommodated fewer than 1,000 passengers. Today, Carnival Corporation consists of six cruise lines: Carnival Cruise Line, Holland America Line, Costa Cruises, Windstar Cruises, Seabourn Cruise Line, and

Cunard Line. In 2001 it operated 43 ships accommodating more than 63,000 passengers — a 32-percent-plus share of the North American market. At the end of 2001 Carnival Corporation had 15 new ships on order (4 for 2002, 4 for 2003, 6 for 2004, and 1 for 2005) that would add more than 34,500 passengers to its capacity.

Carnival and three other major players in the cruise industry together control almost 90 percent of cruise ship capacity. The largest of the three is Royal Caribbean Cruises Limited (RCCL) with a 25-percent market share. RCCL operates two companies: Royal Caribbean International (previously named Royal Caribbean Cruise Line), which in 2001 operated 14 ships, and Celebrity Cruises, purchased in 1997 and operating 9 ships. RCCL plans to add 6 new ships by the end of 2004, raising its capacity from 47,300 to approximately 62,000 passengers.

P&O Princess, the next largest player, is a result of a spin-off by P&O of its cruise lines. P&O Cruises and Princess Cruises were the largest of the six cruise lines operated by P&O. In late 2001 P&O Princess, which was still a relatively new company, became a target for takeover by both RCCL and Carnival Corporation. A merger of P&O Princess and RCCL was announced in November 2001, but Carnival Corporation came forward with a sweeter deal and foiled the arrangement. The matter was put on hold until regulatory agencies in the UK and the USA decided whether a merger with either company would be anti-competitive. P&O Princess operates six cruise lines — P&O Cruises, Princess Cruises, Swan Hellenic Cruises, Aida Cruises, Seetours, and P&O Cruises Australia — which collectively have more 30,000 berths. The company holds a market share of approximately 15 percent and has 7 ships on order, giving it an additional 11,800 berths.

The other major player is Malaysia-based Star Cruises. It expanded in 2000 with the purchase of Norwegian Cruise Line (NCL). After narrowly avoiding a takeover by Carnival Corporation, NCL had bought Majesty Cruise Line in 1997 and Orient Line in 1998. In 2001 the combined company operated three cruise lines — Star Cruises, Norwegian Cruise Line, and Orient Line — with 18 ships having a total of 30,000 berths. Two more ships accommodating a combined 2,000-plus passengers were added in late 2001. Star Cruises' market share is about 15 percent.

When discussing specific cruise lines within this book, I have attempted to use the name that was in effect at the time. Thus, for example, in incidents that occurred prior to the merger in 2000, Princess Cruises remains a separate entity from P&O Cruises; later references are to P&O Princess. Royal Caribbean is variously referred to as Royal Caribbean Cruise Line and Royal Caribbean International.

BIGGER IS BETTER?

Not only are the cruise companies getting bigger, so are the ships. Cruise ships built in the 1970s and before typically accommodated fewer than 1,000 passengers; most held in the range of 600 to 700 passengers. What was considered a large ship back then was one that could accommodate twice that many passengers.

Then, in the 1980s, cruise lines began introducing mega-ships. The first of these, Royal Caribbean Cruise Line's *Sovereign of the Seas*, appeared in 1988, able to accommodate more than 2,800 passengers. Mid-sized ships also grew larger, and by the early 1990s most new ships had berths for between 1,200 and 2,500 passengers.

People had wondered in the late 1980s whether cruise ships could ever get larger than the *Sovereign of the Seas* and its two sister ships. But it wasn't long before new ships plied the waters, 50 to 100 percent larger in physical size and with a passenger capacity exceeding 3,800.

Carnival Cruise Line launched the new wave of mega-ships in 1997 with the introduction of the first Destiny-class ship. The ship was 101,000 tons — compared to the *Sovereign of the Seas* at 73,000 tons — and accommodated 3,400 passengers. Princess Cruises followed in its wake a year later with the *Grand Princess*, physically larger at 109,000 tons but accommodating a "mere" 2,600 passengers.

The largest ships afloat belong to Royal Caribbean International. In 1999 it introduced the *Voyager of the Seas*, the first of several 143,000-ton Eagle-class ships. With accommodations for 3,840 passengers and 1,180 crew members, Eagle-class ships can carry more than 5,000 people.

It is unsurprising that the sheer size of the new cruise ships poses many problems, including increased concerns for passenger safety and security and for the environment. These will be discussed in more detail in Chapters 3 and 4.

ABOUT THIS BOOK

Contrary to most media and industry representations that present positive images of cruising and the cruise industry, the harsh reality is that the cruise industry is neither environmentally nor socially sustainable. In addition, the industry has a history of being misleading in its advertising and in the expectations it sets for consumers. The less-than-positive side has been occasionally identified, but the industry's economic power — a combined annual advertising budget of over $500 million — has been relatively successful at keeping bad press to a minimum. A demonstration of this power followed a 1978 story in the *Sunday Times* that reported American inspectors had found cockroaches and other filth in the galleys of the *Queen Elizabeth 2* and sister Cunard Line ships. In retribution, Cunard Line withdrew $100,000 in advertising from both the *Sunday Times* and the *London Times*.[3]

The industry attitude about the media was made clear at the 2001 World Cruise Tourism Summit in Miami. In the session entitled "Cruise Industry in the Media," several industry executives discussed the politics of media relations. Their view was that there are two types of media: good and bad. The "good media" say good things about the industry; the "bad media" print stories about the industry's underside. Several stories in the *New York Times* written by Douglas Frantz were singled out as exemplars of bad media; the articles discussed environmental assaults by the industry, inadequate medical care on cruise ships, and the vulnerability of passenger and crew to sexual assaults.[4]

The cruise lines' view was that the *New York Times* wanted to tear down the industry and that its reporters systematically searched for data to support that purpose. Michael Crye, president of the International Council of Cruise Lines (ICCL) — the industry's primary lobbyist in Washington — emphasized his point by distributing several media articles. Some purportedly reported the ICCL's position accurately; others purportedly took the same information and presented it in a less than positive light.

The Underside

Cruise Ship Blues: The Underside of the Cruise Industry presents a side of the cruise industry that is rarely discussed. The book begins with two chapters that follow from questions about truth in advertising. Chapter 1 discusses the nature of the industry's advertising and the expectations produced in consumers. The advertised ideal is juxtaposed against the reality. Chapter 2 takes a careful look at the myth of a cruise as an all-inclusive vacation. Most first-time passengers trust cruise-line advertising and happily embark on their cruise expecting few to no expenses not covered by the cruise fare. They are quickly surprised by the multitude of methods used to separate passengers from their money.

Each of the next three chapters looks at issues regarding environmental and social sustainability of the cruise industry. Chapter 3 focuses on safety issues with an examination of the frequency of accidents and breakdowns at sea, and the implications these have for passengers and for the environment. It also considers the security of passengers, the problem of sexual assault, the incidence of food- and airborne illnesses, and inconsistencies in the quality of medical services.

Chapter 4 shifts attention to the cruise industry's environmental record. The many cases of cruise lines polluting the seas have resulted in a collective total of more than $50 million in fines between January 1998 and May 2002. After a glimpse at history, this chapter takes an in-depth look at the nature of the problem, current industry practices, and efforts by coastal states and communities to monitor and regulate the industry. While the industry represents itself as being environmentally friendly, there continue to be cases of pollution by oily bilge water and other harmful emissions.

Chapter 5 completes consideration of the industry's social sustainability by looking at the situation of cruise ship workers. Many are drawn from nonindustrialized countries; those workers who are from industrialized countries are commonly officers or in management positions. This chapter discusses the nature of the work, rates of pay, and commonly found forms of oppression or exploitation.

Chapter 6 shifts attention to the cruise industry's attitude toward its consumers. While the corporate image suggests concern for customer satisfaction and a basic responsiveness to consumers, the fact is that the industry is often consumer unfriendly. This feature is given very little attention in the media, yet the information is critical for anyone who is thinking about taking a cruise.

Chapter 7 takes a step back and considers what can he done — first proposing what could be done by the cruise industry, then examining the types of social and political action that individuals could direct at environmental and social issues. Given the industry's vulnerabilities, what are the prospects for successfully effecting change? This final chapter considers both individual and collective action.

Information Sources

The information within this book is drawn from a range of sources. The largest source is my experiences as a cruise passenger. I had taken several cruises as a youngster, and in 1992 naively took to cruising as a vacation choice. My experiences provide firsthand knowledge of the many facets of cruising and onboard life.

As a sociologist, I was at first intrigued with the social life and social problems aboard cruise ships. Then, as I went on more and more cruises, I began to uncover the underside of shipboard life, to document common issues or problems, and to explore in greater depth some of the items that appeared in the media. My time aboard ships has afforded opportunities to meet and get to know crew, staff, and onboard managers. As a consumer, I demand honesty from providers of products and services; if I feel what is delivered is less than has been promised, the responsible company is sure to know about it. Given this predisposition, it is unsurprising that I also gained alarming insight into corporate attitudes of cruise lines and the strategies they use in dealing with consumers.

Overall, I have spent more than 300 days on cruise ships. I have sailed with all of the major cruise lines, traveling in both a range of classes on ships and a range of classes of ships.

I've added print research to this body of firsthand experience, including media reports; government hearings, investigations, and reports; position papers and publications from industry organizations and individual cruise lines; trade publications; and reports and studies from environmental groups and labor organizations. I have also attended the industry's annual convention and trade show, the Seatrade Cruise Shipping Convention, gaining wide access after being granted a press pass.

Where possible, the source of sensitive information is identified. In some cases, particularly those involving an employee who is vulnerable to retribution for honest sharing of information, the source remains confidential.

What you are about to read may at times seem unbelievable. At other times it may be depressing. Either way, the goal of this book is to bring to the forefront information that has been kept underground and to provide the foundation for social and political action and, ultimately, for needed change in an industry that has, for the most part, avoided close scrutiny.

ONBOARD THE FLOATING RESORT

IMAGINE SWIMMING IN CRYSTAL-CLEAR AQUAMARINE WATER, parasailing in the warm Caribbean sunshine, lounging on a pristine, vacuum-cleaned white sand beach, being artistically served visually pleasing meals, having your every whim anticipated and catered to, and being treated to a different, extravagant Las Vegas-style show every night. These are images of what to expect from a cruise vacation.

Cruises are advertised as the perfect idyllic vacation. The image is reflected by television shows set onboard cruise ships, by advertisements, and by glossy cruise-line brochures. Each gives a sense of how you will be indulged in opulence, pampered in luxury.

The images are certainly inviting: cruise lines are selling a product. Like any effective marketing campaign, the goal is to make the product to appeal to the widest possible audience. Each person is given something meaningful, something that makes the cruise experience seem attractive to him or her. The obvious question is, can it truly be that good?

TELL THEM WHAT THEY WANT TO HEAR

"The Love Boat" television show gave many of us our first image of cruising: the socially affable captain, the all-American crew, the cruise director who knew everyone's name and who took an active interest in everyone's lives, the abundance of single people aboard looking for love. I saw the original episodes as a youngster and assumed, like everyone else, that the image presented was accurate.

In 1997, when I took a cruise on the original Love Boat, the *Pacific Princess*, several episodes of "The Love Boat" were aired on one of the ship's television stations. The contrast between television and reality was staggering. What struck me first was the difference in the passenger cabins. On the TV show, they were nicely appointed and about as large as a typical hotel room, with a double or queen-size bed. My room aboard the *Pacific Princess*, on the other hand, was 130 square feet — at most, one-third the size of rooms shown on the television show — with a bathroom no larger than a closet. I slept on a smaller-than-average twin bed, with my feet hanging over the end. No passenger cabin on this ship had a double or queen-size bed.

The contrast between television and reality carried over to the dining room. On the TV show, passengers sat at tables with whoever they wished, went to dinner whenever they wanted, had long, leisurely meals with the freedom to take a spin around the dance floor between courses, and the dining room was spacious. In reality, dining times were rigidly set, you were assigned to dine with the same people at the same table every night, there was no dance floor, and space between tables was sufficient but not ample. Unlike on the show, none of the officers or service staff were American. That the experience was a reality check is an understatement.

Like No Vacation on Earth

The nature of the cruise industry's advertising has changed significantly over the past decade. In the 1980s and early 1990s, advertisements commonly focused on the cruise ship and the cruise experience. Images shown concretely represented what to expect when going on a cruise, from the physical facilities to the abundance of food.

In the mid-1990s the focus of ads began to shift. Norwegian Cruise Line was the first to develop an advertising campaign with a strong emotional appeal and using abstract images. Their "It's Different Out Here" campaign, which was criticized by many in the industry for not effectively selling the advertised product, received several awards (including a CLIO, a Kelly Award, and an award from the One Club of New York) for its creativity. As well, the print campaign scored higher than average in readers' memory of seeing the ad in a particular issue of a publication and on noting who the advertiser was.

Other cruise lines soon followed Norwegian Cruise Line's lead. The result is that today much advertising is abstract and based on emotional appeal. Carnival Cruise Line — for a long time associated with images of Kathie Lee Gifford singing "If My Friends Could See Me Now" while having a fabulous time aboard a ship — introduced a series of advertisements with dancing fish and dancing palm trees, projecting the company's moniker "The Fun Ship." More recent ads show passengers post-cruise telling viewers about the great time they had and building up the virtues of Carnival Cruise Line.

Carnival Cruise Line and Norwegian Cruise Line are not alone in attempting to appeal to consumers' emotions through their ad campaigns. Celebrity Cruises sails under the slogan "Exceeding Expectations," Royal Caribbean suggests its cruises are "Like No Vacation on Earth," and the Cruise Line International Association (CLIA) — the industry's joint marketing arm — claims "You Haven't Lived Until You've Cruised." Norwegian Cruise Line has "Freestyle Cruising"; Princess Cruises, "Personal Choice Cruising"; and Costa Cruises, "Cruising Italian Style." All of these slogans produce images that are positive but nonspecific.

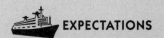 **EXPECTATIONS**

Although cruise-line promotional campaigns generally favor an emotional appeal, overall the cruise industry "hasn't done a good job of figuring out what the consumer is looking for when they take a cruise on an emotional level and delivering on that," according to a Renaissance Cruises vice-president.[1] The cruise line's advertisement creates a non-specific but very concrete expectation in the consumer's mind. And therein lies the problem: the highly individual and personal nature of customer expectations makes it unlikely that the cruise line will be able to live up to what it appears to have promised.

Back Down to Earth

Celebrity Cruises' slogan, "Exceeding Expectations," is a good example of the problem with emotional appeal. How can a company promise to exceed everybody's expectations? It sets people up for disappointment. In 1995 I went on a Celebrity cruise, naively buying into their promise — I truly expected them to exceed my expectations. But sadly, they did not.

The problem of high expectations is compounded by Celebrity's advertising "Michel Roux cuisine." Michel Roux, a Michelin-starred chef operates the Waterside Inn in Bray, England (just outside London). For a hefty consulting fee — reported by some industry insiders to be as high as $1 million a year — he directs the cruise line on menu and recipe development, periodically visits ships, and lends his name to the product. The food is not comparable to what you would find at a Michelin-starred restaurant, but then, you wouldn't expect it to be.

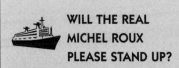

WILL THE REAL MICHEL ROUX PLEASE STAND UP?

Celebrity Cruise's advertising is confusing: there are two chefs named Michel Roux. One is Michel Roux, chef at the Waterside Inn near London. His nephew, also named Michel Roux, is chef de cuisine at Le Gavroche, a Michelin-starred restaurant in London's Mayfair district. You may well ask, which restaurant represents "Michel Roux cuisine"?

Despite the hype, Celebrity's food is not much different from that of other cruise lines in its class. My Celebrity Cruise experience included lettuce that showed visible rusting, bruised and discolored fruit, cartilage and gristle as "edible" parts of boneless chicken, soups that were thin and flavorless, and food that was generally on par with a banquet at a mid-scale hotel. I wrote to the company and was told that my comments would be passed along to Apollo Ship Chandlers, the concessionaire providing the company's food service. Nothing else was ever heard.

The newest wave in product development and advertising is "freestyle cruising" and "personal choice cruising." The concepts are inviting: passengers are told they can dine where they want, when they want, and with whoever they want. However, it is not uncommon for dining rooms to be full and for passengers to have to wait a substantial amount of time before being seated. In the case of Princess Cruises, passengers can request traditional dining (with a set time and table) or personal choice dining (dine when they want). Given an overdemand for traditional dining, many passengers are, against their wishes, assigned the personal choice option.

Emotional appeals extend to other facets of the cruise experience. Most of these exhibit similar differences between the expectations produced and the product delivered, including for entertainment, service, and the overall quality of the cruise experience.

THIS ISN'T THE CRUISE I WAS PROMISED

One of my biggest struggles on cruises was reconciling the incongruity between image and reality. All cruise-line brochures claim the best food at sea, the best entertainment, the most varied schedule of activities, and staff that provide impeccable personal service. The reality is that differences between cruise lines in the same general class — that is, mass-market, premium, or ultraluxury — tend to be insignificant. Entertainment is good but rarely great. Activities are varied but pretty much identical from one cruise line to the next. And service reflects the standards set by management on a particular ship more than standards set by the company: the same company can provide a wide variation between its many ships. But in my experience, the areas with the greatest gap between image and reality are food and accommodations.

Five-Star Dining Every Night

All cruise lines make grand claims about their food. Claims about food being bountiful are accurate, but claims about quality are often overblown. This is unsurprising, given the amount cruise lines budget for food. Mass-market cruise lines, such as Carnival Cruise Line and Royal Caribbean, typically spend between $10 and $11 per passenger per day. Premium cruise lines, such as Holland America Line and Celebrity Cruises, spend $12 to $15 per passenger per day, on average. Ultraluxury cruise lines, such as Seabourn Cruise Line, Silversea Cruises, and Radisson Seven Seas Cruises, spend from $20 to $24 per passenger per day.[2]

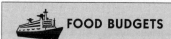 **FOOD BUDGETS**

Industry-wide, it was estimated that in 1994 the average spent for food, per passenger per day, was $12.[3] With the increased buying power of larger companies and greater efficiencies of scale, cruise line food budgets have either remained static or decreased.[4]

Within these parameters, there is, obviously, a limit to the quality that can be provided. The best meals I have had on a cruise ship were only comparable to what you would find at a mid-range hotel restaurant. The majority of meals were equivalent to food that might be served at a large banquet. People returning from a cruise seldom express this view — most are, I think, embarrassed to admit their disappointment.

Given the sheer scale of food production — a mid-sized ship serves 1,500 to 1,800 three- or four-course meals every evening, and a large ship serves twice that number — various shortcuts would be expected. Cruise lines increasingly use pre-packaged foods, including canned soups, pre-cut and pre-sized portions, and frozen desserts. Much of your dinner is prepared in advance and kept either under heat lamps or in food warmers. In almost every case, all that is added before delivery from the galley to your table are last-minute finishing touches.

Cruise-line food is certainly palatable, but the discerning diner will experience many disappointments. Egg product is commonly used instead of fresh eggs; poached eggs may be made in mass, then refrigerated, and later reheated by dipping in hot water immediately before serving; salad greens are often wilted or showing signs of rust from sitting too long in the refrigerator; and a concentrate consisting of 77 percent water and 23 percent "coffee-based dry matter" is often used for coffee. Do not assume that real ground coffee will be served.

Trusting menu descriptions may produce similar disappointments. On a premium cruise line, a "classic Caesar" salad came with iceberg lettuce; on an ultraluxury cruise line, the same menu item was served with rosemary-flavored croutons. A "spinach salad" on a premium cruise line was served with a single spinach leaf atop a bed of iceberg lettuce; a "watercress salad" on an ultraluxury cruise line had no watercress. The list could go on: sorrel soup with no sorrel, cannoli with rancid mascarpone cheese, lobster bisque with no lobster, Caribbean black bean soup that resembled a minestrone with a couple of black beans thrown in. The first couple of times you might overlook these deficiencies, but with repetition you learn to not trust the menu. You place your order and you take your chances.

Food service is also below standards common to mid-scale or upscale restaurants onshore. If you believe that good service is fast service, then a cruise is a perfect choice. On most ships meals are forced into slots of 90 minutes (give or take 15 minutes) from the time you are seated to the time you are escorted out the door. Courses are served in sequence, but they are not coordinated so that everyone at the table is served the same course at the same time.

The norm, even on cruise lines where there is no need to rush a person out of the dining room, is to serve the next course as soon as the previous course is finished. I recently sailed on an ultraluxury cruise ship where there was open seating (meaning no one was waiting for the table to be vacated). Frequently my plate was removed as soon as I put my fork down — even while I was still chewing — with a new plate appearing before I had swallowed. If I took my time before beginning the next course, I was asked whether everything was all right.

You'll see things on cruise ships that would never be seen, much less tolerated, at a restaurant on land. On both Norwegian Cruise Line and Holland America Line, I watched an assistant maitre d' assist passengers by removing their lobster tail from the shell. In both cases, this employee went from table to

 THE *RADISSON DIAMOND*'S GRAND DINING ROOM

On the ultraluxury *Radisson Diamond*, the same waiters that served my partner and me were also serving a table of senior officers and VIPs. Their mineral water was poured from a bottle wrapped in a white napkin; our mineral water — the same brand — was poured without the napkin.

We watched as they were served their entree: a whole sea bass weighing about eight pounds. The fish was brought out on a tray and carved at their table: a very nice touch — except that our table had a fish head (with its open mouth and eyes) staring us in the face (no more than four feet away) from the time the fish was presented until their table had finished their entree. Our table had the unpleasant experience of the extremely fishy smell, and we had to watch as the assistant maitre d' cleaned the fish bones in front of us, at the end pulling the full ribcage into the air from the tail and holding what was left vertically before taking it away to the garbage.

Ultraluxury? I don't think so!

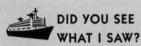
DID YOU SEE WHAT I SAW?

In the atrium of Princess Cruise's *Pacific Princess*, several assistant maitre d's were setting up a champagne waterfall. They had finished building the one-story-high pyramid and had sprayed the glasses with champagne. As they were placing grapes in the glasses, a passenger came by and asked to take a picture. One of the assistant maitre d's posed for the picture, placing a grape in his mouth as though it was an apple in the mouth of a pig. The picture was taken, the passenger turned and walked away, and the assistant maitre d' took the grape from his mouth and flicked it into a champagne glass. My partner and I turned, looked at each other, and simultaneously said, "Did you see what I saw?"

table, passenger to passenger, using the same knife and fork on almost 100 plates. He'd wave the silverware around, accidentally rub it against his and others' clothing, and frequently touch seat backs with the knife and fork as he talked to passengers.

Granted, these types of occurrences are not commonplace, but they happen often enough. But if a similar situation happened just once at an onshore restaurant, most people would choose not to return. If you complained to management at that onshore restaurant, the matter would be addressed and an effort made to retain your patronage. When these situations happen at sea, however, the passenger is often viewed as the problem for having complained. The behavior continues.

Why do people keep going on cruises if these types of occurrences are so common? In most cases, the problems are not even acknowledged or else they are ignored. This is illustrated by a comment a fellow passenger on the ultraluxury *Seabourn Goddess I* made in response to dismal service at lunch. Although he and his wife were visibly upset and dissatisfied, when I attempted to commiserate, he excused the major lapses in service by simply saying, "They are doing the best that they can." He fully intended to take a future cruise with the same cruise line.

I Booked This Cabin and This Is the Cabin I Want

Cruise ship accommodations are quite different from the pictures in advertisements and brochures. The contrast was made abundantly clear to me on Royal Caribbean Cruise Line in 1993. I was walking by the purser's desk and overheard a fellow passenger pointing to the picture in a brochure and saying quite loudly, "I booked this cabin and this is the cabin I want." The picture in the brochure, taken with a wide-angle lens, made the man's 140-square-foot room look roomy and spacious — at least two or three times larger than it actually was. I was envious. His room was almost 20 percent larger than mine.

Actual room size is confronted by almost everyone taking his or her first cruise. Brochures display images and descriptions that give the impression of a decent-sized hotel room. Very few brochures indicate the actual square footage of the room.

You quickly learn that rooms may be as small as 120 square feet, in standard categories are often between 140 and 160 square feet, and are rarely — unless a mini-suite or a suite — larger than 190 to 200 square feet, including the bathroom and the closets.

To put this into perspective, a typical queen-size bed is about 40 square feet — it occupies 20 to 33 percent of the room. When you add a dresser, a desk and chair, and perhaps a couch and bookshelf, there is little room to maneuver. Passengers on Royal Caribbean International, known to have some of the smallest standard rooms, often comment that the bathroom is so small that it can accommodate only one person at a time. Full-sized individuals complain that using the toilet or the shower is a challenge.

At the other extreme are the suites found on many ships. Although still smaller than a suite in a hotel — often equivalent in size to a standard hotel room — they can be comfortable. Many suites are 500 square feet; a penthouse suite may be two or three times that size. Some can be ostentatious, such as the villas on Norwegian Cruise Lines' new ship, the *Norwegian Star*. Standard cabins on this ship range in size from 160 to 172 square feet; the villa provides an astounding 5,300 square feet.

I DIDN'T KNOW I WAS IN STEERAGE CLASS

Cruise lines advertise that classes on cruise ships are something of the past. Oceangoing vessels used to have two or three classes (first class, steerage, and so on) and based on their class of service, passengers were restricted in where they were permitted to go on the ship. Although today's ships are represented as being class-

THE BIGGEST SUITES AFLOAT

The *Norwegian Star* offers the most incredible suites you will ever find on a cruise ship. At 5,300 square feet each, the Garden Villas are the cruise industry's largest accommodations.

Each three-bedroom villa has a contemporary living/dining room with a grand piano, flat-screen TV/VCR, and a desk equipped with a laptop computer, printer/fax, and a modem. Each bedroom, decorated in rich colors with Asian paintings and Japanese prints, has its own dressing room and walk-in closets as well as an en suite bathroom with floor-to-ceiling windows, a whirlpool tub, separate shower, double sinks, and a television. One bedroom opens onto a Japanese garden with decorative pools, a small bridge, sunny and shaded seating areas, and a Jacuzzi. A staircase leads up to a large expanse of open deck overlooking the ship's pool area.

The suite even comes with a stainless steel butler's pantry, which is used for in-suite food and beverage service. It is particularly useful when the occupants wish to host dinner parties or cocktail parties in their room.

free, many class distinctions nevertheless remain.

You Get What You Pay For

I first became aware of onboard class differences when, on a Royal Caribbean Cruise Line ship, I noticed that passengers in rooms on the deck above mine were given different colored (and plusher) towels than those given to me. The point was driven home several years later on Royal Cruise Line when I was unexpectedly upgraded to the Owner's Suite. I learned that it isn't just towels that vary based on one's room. Bathroom amenities — shampoo, body lotion, soaps, slippers, and so on — vary in both number and quality between different classes of cabin. As well, preference in accessing activities (including alternative restaurants) and in assignment of dining room tables is often given to those in more expensive rooms. These passengers are given first choice of tables in the alternative restaurant and the most favorable tables in the main dining room.

Holland America Line, for example, not only has a private dining room and private lounge for its passengers residing in suites, it also gives suite passengers priority seating in its alternative restaurant, and its two-level dining room is stratified based on class of cabins: those in more expensive cabins sit on the upper level, those in cheaper cabins are seated on the lower level. Passengers with more expensive rooms are also more likely to be invited to VIP parties and receptions or to the captain's (or other officer's) table for dinner, and they will be provided with more personalized service. None of this is surprising, but it is inconsistent with the egalitarian image that cruise lines project.

You Don't Get What You Pay For

Like hotels and restaurants and other aspects of the hospitality industry in general, cruise lines themselves are stratified into classes. Curiously, these class differences are not always consistent with differences in pricing. In fact, very often you'll pay the same price for equivalent accommodations on a mass-market cruise line as you would on a premium cruise line. But the product advertised is quite different, and the product received may also vary. One key difference between ships in these categories is the cruise line's budgets for food and for activities, and the ratio of staff to passengers. Premium cruise lines tend to have more workers per passenger than cruise lines in the lower categories. The largest ships afloat are in the mass-market category.

"Present management favors financial rather than market driven decisions. This spurs short term decisions that will, over time, weaken cruising's appeal to consumers. Consumers are no longer told how great it is to sail, but how great the sale is."[5]
— Michael Grossman, Cruise Industry News Quarterly

The greatest difference is between cruise lines in the ultraluxury category and the others. Ultraluxury ships are smaller and have more staff per passenger — sometimes the ratio approaches one to one. As well, you'll enjoy meals that are prepared to order rather than mass-produced.

Although the ultraluxury product may be of higher quality, there are still major gaps between image and reality. Seabourn Cruise Line, for example, recently introduced the concept of "Seabourn Refined" — the latter word touted as being both a noun and a verb. Advertisements promise fine Egyptian cotton towels and being treated to random indulgences, perhaps a spritz of water or an ice-chilled facecloth bestowed while you are lying in the sun, or a mini-massage provided while you lounge on deck. In my experience, however, Royal Velvet in New York City made the towels and the "random indulgences" were so random as to be practically nonexistent.

Seabourn is not alone in making unfulfilled promises. Like other cruise lines in the ultraluxury category, Seabourn provides passengers complimentary wines at meals — although, also like other cruise lines, some of these wines are unpalatable to even the most basic of tastes. Silversea Cruises, reputed to be the ultimate in cruising, at one point limited the complimentary wines to those with a wholesale cost of no more than $2 a bottle. Based on its December 2001 offerings, Seabourn has a similar budget. Curiously, the company doesn't offer wines comparable to what their upscale clientele might drink at home.[6] On a cruise aboard the *Seabourn Goddess I*, a passenger remarked that the brand of Rioja wine served one night was the same one his mother bought in milk cartons to use as a cooking wine.

Uncompromising service is another promise made in advertising by ultraluxury cruise lines. The reality can fall very short. In Chapter 6 I describe an experience on the *Radisson Diamond* that is best summarized as Radisson's "no, I can't" attitude rather than its promised "yes, I can" attitude. Music was played at a bar, apparently for the entertainment of staff rather than passengers — these particular passengers were unlikely to regularly listen to rap. Attempts to change the situation led to increasingly passive-aggressive behavior by a bar waiter toward the passengers who complained. Similarly, on the *Seabourn Goddess* I, I advised the hotel manager of several lapses in service. He spoke to the staff, but also told them who had made the comments. Several waiters provided my partner and me with poor service thereafter, and one refused to provide any service at all.

The promise of quality service by ultraluxury companies can be compromised by the ship's small size. Many of these ships accommodate as few as 200 to 400 passengers. The small size of the ship results in the impression that passengers are essentially coming into the staff's home. And just as it is considered poor manners to complain when invited to a friend's house for dinner, the service providers in these small settings are offended if passengers are not appreciative of everything they do. They resent passengers who complain and will collectively sanction anyone who is not unconditionally appreciative. Trust me, the ship is small enough for this to happen. Corporate management appears to support this behavior, despite its stark contrast to the advertised promises.

HERE'S A QUARTER SO YOU CAN CALL SOMEONE WHO CARES

If you believe the advertising by cruise lines, you're bound to be disappointed. Some cruise industry insiders confess that they expect from 5 to 10 percent of passengers to leave a cruise dissatisfied — but few of those people express their disappointment. Many passengers simply assume their expectations were too high — forgetting that it was the cruise line's own advertising that shaped those expectations.

My partner and I meet many "cruise apologists" — people who at sea are willing to accept reduced service and reduced quality, yet on land are inflexible and demanding. The cruise ship is a unique entity that effectively stifles dissatisfaction, and that skillfully turns problems around so passengers are made to feel that the problem is them rather than the situation or service.

Another way that the cruise industry deals with customer complaints is through its cruise contract or "Terms of Passage," a standard form which is provided to passengers after they've paid for their cruise. The contract states that acceptance of the ticket — which at that point, is nonrefundable — constitutes acceptance of the terms of the contract.

The contract absolves the cruise line of responsibility for the actions of concessionaires — another little-known fact is that most ships have many concessionaires who provide specific onboard services, such as photography or medical care — and, except within very tight guidelines, for its own actions.

This fact was driven home quite painfully several years ago on a cruise in the southern Caribbean. One night at dinner I chewed down on a shard of ceramic pottery that was mixed in the chocolate-cappuccino mousse. I immediately brought the matter to the attention of management, and the next morning, because of a toothache, I visited the ship's physician to file a report.

CRUISE CONTRACT

Excerpts of Contract Terms and Conditions of Transportation

- The ship's schedule and itinerary may change or be changed without any liability to the Carrier.

[A port call may be shortened or canceled. Don't expect compensation.]

- The Carrier is not liable for any personal injury or death unless caused by the Carrier's negligence without any contributory negligence by the Passenger.

[If you slip and fall, that may be considered contributory negligence.]

- The Carrier is not liable for any personal injury or death caused by any physician, dentist, nurse, or medical technician, or by any concessionaire unless the Carrier negligently retained such person. All such persons, entities, are independent contractors.

[It is helpful to know which onboard services — including food service — are provided by a concessionaire.]

- The Carrier is not liable for loss or damage to Passenger's personal effects, baggage, and property unless caused solely by the Carrier's negligence and in no event will the Carrier's liability exceed the sum of $500 for loss or damage to all such items. The Carrier is not liable for

After I returned home, I learned that the tooth was cracked and required a triple root canal. I contacted the cruise company and asked how to proceed with a claim for my dental bills. My first and second contacts were ignored. The response to my third contact, made directly to the company's president, was that the matter was between their concessionaire and me; they had no responsibility or liability. They didn't tell me the name of the concessionaire nor who to contact. Four months later, following abusive treatment by the concessionaire (who I had tracked down on my own), I had to threaten legal action — a threat apparently viewed as credible, given that I have a relative who practices law in the city where the company is located — before finally being reimbursed any such loss or damage unless written notice thereof is given to the ship's purser before the Passenger disembarks, and written notice thereof is also given ... *[to the cruise line's head* office] within three days after the Passenger disembarks.

[A passenger whose laundry was accidentally incinerated by a cruise line had his claim limited to $150 even though the value of the destroyed clothing was more than $1,650.]

- The Carrier is not liable for any other claim unless written notice is given to ... [the cruise line's head office] within fifteen days after the claim arose, and the Carrier is not liable for any other suit unless instituted against the Carrier with three months after the claim arose.

[The contract specifies the court in which a lawsuit must be filed.]

- Shore excursions are not operated by the Carrier. The Carrier is not responsible for the performance of shore excursions or for any losses, injuries, or damages occurring ashore whether during an organized excursion or otherwise.

[The cruise line is not responsible for the port of call sightseeing tours it sells en route.]

Source: Celebrity Cruises (1995). Note: The clauses of the above contract are typical of those provided by other cruise lines.

for my dental bills. In return for the meager compensation, I had to trade away my ability to name the companies involved.

The attitude of cruise lines toward customer relations is discussed further in Chapter 6. As you will see, the level of responsiveness to my cracked tooth was actually better than the norm.

NEXT TIME YOU SEE A CRUISE AD ...

Think about what you have just read the next time you see an advertisement for a cruise. Be aware of the expectations being created by the ad and wonder whether those expectations can be realized. Is the product being accurately represented? Do you really think you will have the experience being promised?

THE MYTH OF THE
ALL-INCLUSIVE VACATION

Scene: Onboard Norwegian Cruise Line's Dreamward, *Fort Lauderdale, Florida, the last morning of the cruise.*

As everyone is leaving the ship, a young man with a bad sunburn squirms uncomfortably at the reception desk, feverishly trying to find some way to pay the $500 tab he had run up during the one-week cruise. He didn't have any credit cards, he'd already tried to get money wired from home, and he was faced with not being allowed off the ship until the bill was paid in full. The unhappy young man had no idea how he had spent that much money.[1]

ONE OF THE MOST MISLEADING IDEAS presented in cruise-line advertising is that a cruise is all-inclusive. Some ads and many brochures explicitly state that all-inclusiveness is a key advantage of a cruise over other vacations. However, there are subtle contradictions to this claim. Consider the Royal Caribbean International ad using the line, "It's More Than a Cruise." Images show the things you could do on a cruise, but what's left unsaid is that for every one of those activities there is an additional charge.

Most passengers assume there will be no major expenses beyond their cruise fare. Although it is possible to not spend a penny more, it's not easy. The list of activities and items with extra charges is quite long and getting longer all the time. Like the young man in the opening scene, many people end a cruise with a bill that is much higher than they dreamed possible. I know a couple who won a free seven-day cruise in 1999. At the end of the week, their bill for onboard expenses was $1,800. They hadn't dreamed they had spent that much.

Consumers are drawn to advertising that promotes a cruise as a relatively inexpensive vacation. And granted, adjusting for inflation, the cost of a cruise is considerably less today than it was 5, 10, or even 20 years ago. Yet over those years, the income generated by cruise lines has consistently increased. In January 2002 Micky Arison, chief executive officer of Carnival Corporation, suggested that at the current stage of the industry's growth cycle, which is in the midst of a four-year expansion, increased income is unlikely to be achieved from price increases.[2] Instead, it will be derived from "operational efficiency" — that is, cutting costs — and increased onboard revenue. Onboard revenue includes all money passengers spend onboard the ship, including in the bars, shops, casinos, and much more.

Onboard revenue has the largest impact on the cruise line's economic bottom line. The company can practically give away a cruise and still make a profit. Exact figures for onboard revenue are difficult to come by, but Festival Cruises concedes that one-third of its revenues come from "additional spending" — which means that whatever you pay for your cruise, you're expected to spend one-third again onboard the ship. Once in port, further income is generated from shore excursions.[3]

> "Modern cruise ships are little more than floating bedfactories with shops and restaurants attached. Time spent at sea is simply a matter of getting from A to B with an emphasis on cajoling those trapped inside into spending their money on shopping, drinks, and other extras."[5]
>
> — Jon Ashworth, London Times

Comments by Wall Street analysts during the competition between Carnival Corporation and Star Cruises for the takeover of Norwegian Cruise Line provided a rare glimpse at the amount generated by onboard spending. It was suggested that Norwegian Cruise Line had lower than average levels of onboard revenue, which in 1999 was between $220 and $233 per person, per day.[4]

HOW TO GENERATE INCOME ... LET ME COUNT THE WAYS

For many people, it's hard to imagine how you could spend $220 or more a day aboard a cruise ship. True, most passengers do not spend this much. The figure is an average — which means there are some people who spend much, much more. What do they spend their money on? The largest sources of onboard revenue are casinos, bars, and, most recently, art auctions.

Traditional Sources of Onboard Revenue

Strategies for generating onboard revenue first appeared in the late 1970s and early 1980s with establishment of a "Corporate Manager of Onboard Revenue." Cruise lines have always provided shopping, a service normally contracted to a concessionaire. But then they realized there were other ways to generate income. Some money generators, such as bingo — previously run by the cruise director with the profits either remaining in his or her pocket or being shared with the cruise staff — were brought under the company's control.

Cruise lines also introduced a system of approved stores at ports. This brought into the corporate coffers income that had previously been paid under the table to the cruise director or the port lecturer. The amounts generated are not trivial. A cruise director could make as much as $250,000 a year in under-the-table kickbacks. Under the new scheme of cruise line-approved stores, in 1994 an upscale store on St. Thomas in the US Virgin Islands paid as much as $700 per port call to be listed in the promotional materials distributed to passengers on a large ship ("large" meaning one with 1,200 to 1,500 passengers). In 1994 1.24 million cruise ship passengers visited that port, each spending $372 on average.[6] In 2001 St. Thomas received more than 1.8 million cruise passengers; average spending was $173 per person. (Changes in the demographics of the typical cruise passenger over the past decade account for decreased spending.)

REVENUES

Lloyd's List reported in 1997 that Princess Cruises' *Sun Princess*, with 1,200 passengers, generated $6 million a week in onboard revenue.

Drink Up — You Won't Feel a Thing

One of top three income generators is the ship's bars. In the early 1970s cruises had a reputation for providing cheap drinks. Between purchasing liquor at duty-free prices and the cruise ship bars making a marginal attempt to generate income, a mixed drink could be had for as little as 35 to 50 cents. But once liquor became seen as a source of income, prices increased considerably. In the late 1980s a drink cost $1.50 to $2.00; in 2002 the same drink costs between $4.00 and $7.50.

Cruise lines use a range of strategies to increase bar revenue. Some ships offer a drink as you embark. Unsuspecting passengers take a drink from a tray and are immediately asked to sign so the charge can be added to their shipboard account. Most people are too embarrassed to give the drink back; they have been had. The traditional sail-away party on deck is similarly used. Waiters wander through the crowd with watered-down, pre-mixed beverages, offering them to everyone they pass. During the cruise itself, consumption is further encouraged with specialty drinks — the "drink of the day" — provided at promotional prices. The drink of the day is often served in a souvenir glass, which justifies a premium price.

 **DRINK UP**

Cruise lines expect 20 percent of revenues from beverage sales to represent actual costs for the product.[8]

Theme nights are another method for encouraging purchases at the bar. A number of years ago, one company capitalized on the popularity of line dancing, and replaced the traditional midnight tropical fruit buffet with a country-and-western theme buffet. Passengers who had previously come to the buffet for a quick look or to sample some fruit began staying longer and either joining in or watching the line dancing. As a result, bar revenue increased by $1.10 per passenger, which on a 2,000-passenger ship sailing 50 weeks a year meant an annual increase of $110,000. In addition, the cruise ship saved $50,000 a year due to lower food costs for the western theme buffet.[7]

No Competition — You Must Buy from Us

In the mid-1990s cruise lines began preventing passengers from bringing aboard their own wine, liquor, beer, soft drinks, or bottled water. Anything that is brought onboard at embarkation or during a port call can be confiscated by the ship, to be returned at the end of the cruise. This policy is designed to ensure that passengers wanting a drink will purchase their beverages from the ship — the equivalent of a hotel requiring guests who want a beverage to use the minibar or room service.

The explanations given by cruise lines for this policy omit the real agenda. A spokesperson for Norwegian Cruise Lines, probably the most restrictive of those serving the mass market, suggests:

> A big part of this is really to have control of minors getting ahold of alcohol.... In years past there have been some situations where we have had underage drinking going on, and those passengers were disruptive.[9]

Royal Caribbean similarly claimed that its policy of restricting the bringing aboard of liquor was a means of reducing the likelihood

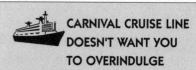 **CARNIVAL CRUISE LINE DOESN'T WANT YOU TO OVERINDULGE**

Although Carnival Cruise Line has a strictly enforced ban on passengers bringing aboard any alcohol at any time, the company knows that the odd bottle arrives on the ship undetected. "But you're not going to get away with bringing in a large volume of drinks at a port of call. We're going to take it from you and give it back to you at the end of the cruise," said a Carnival spokesperson.

If you drink in your cabin, so be it — that's your business.... *There are some guests who would interpret that as meaning it is OK to bring large quantities of liquor on board, and then that leads to issues of disruptive behavior. If you're buying it on board at typical prices, it's likely that you're not going to consume as much as if you had 10 cases of beer in your cabin.*[12]

It is difficult not to be cynical: passengers should be thankful the cruise line looks so carefully after their interest. After all, $84.00 is a small price to pay for a case of beer (24 bottles at $3.50 each) to ensure that you don't overindulge. At these prices, it's obvious why bars are such a large source of onboard revenue.

that minors would get their hands on it. Interestingly, that company expressed a different view in 1994 after a 14-year-old boy died with a blood-alcohol level of 0.29. He had been supplied with a bottle's worth of tequila and rum in a two-hour period by a 24-year-old fellow passenger. At the time Royal Caribbean expressed no responsibility, stating: "A cruise is a resort vacation. It's not a babysitting service."[10] In January 2002 the company reduced the onboard drinking age from 21 to 18 when in international waters or at a port where it is legal to drink at that age.[11]

Why Not Mix That Drink with a Test of Your Luck?

Casinos are another major source of onboard revenue.[13] Like bar sales, this income source is relatively recent. Prior to the 1980s, you couldn't take it for granted that there would be a casino onboard your cruise ship. Ships that did have gambling had a small number of slot machines — between 20 and 40 on average — and perhaps a roulette wheel, a craps table, and a blackjack table, all tucked into a small, out-of-the way room.

By the 1990s shipboard casinos not only became commonplace, but considerable competition existed for having the biggest or the best casino afloat. On some ships the casino has two or three floors and 100 to 400 or more slot machines. Other ships offer settings comparable to any top-of-the-line Las Vegas-style casino. Cruise-line brochures often display images of glamour and glitz in casinos at sea.

As in Las Vegas and Atlantic City, the concessionaires operating cruise ship casinos use various strategies to draw people in. Some offer free cruises to players who agree to a minimum (high) level of gambling. Different strategies are used to attract passengers who are not "high-rollers." Almost all cruise ship casinos offer free champagne or cocktails the first or second night of the cruise to draw people in and to familiarize them with what's available. Free lessons and/or a limited number of "free play" or "match play" chips may be offered to get people started, and tournaments are staged to attract others.

These strategies not only attract people interested in gambling, but also those who like to watch others test their luck. Undoubtedly, many observers become novice gamblers. I watched one man lose $500 in under an hour as he learned to play roulette. I met another man who said he expected to lose $15,000 during his 50-day circumnavigation of South America.

We Have It All — At Duty-Free Prices

There was a time when the shops onboard a cruise ship provided only a minimum of items. You could buy any toiletries and sundries that you had forgotten to pack, a few souvenir items with the ship's and cruise line's logo, and a limited selection of duty-free liquor and tobacco products. Over the years the selection of items has increased, as has the amount of space allotted for onboard shops.

Almost all onboard shops are run by one of two concessionaires: Greyhound Leisure Services' International Cruise Ships Division, which in the year 2000 served 77 ships, and Miami Cruise Line Services (owned by Louis Vuitton Moët Hennessy), which has shops on 100 ships spanning 26 different cruise lines.

Norwegian Cruise Line's *Norway* was one of the first ships to introduce a collection of shops. On its enclosed promenade deck, passengers can stroll along "streets" called Champs-Elysées and Fifth Avenue, where shops and boutiques offer everything from mink coats and diamonds to costume jewelry and casual sportswear. The *Norway*'s success encouraged similar development on other ships. The most lavish collection of shops was on Cunard Line's *QE 2*, which offered a seagoing branch of Harrods department store and included boutique names such as Gucci, Alfred Dunhill, Christian Dior, Louis Vuitton, and H. Stern. You could buy almost anything aboard the ship.

While this scale was unique in the early 1990s, on today's ships it is commonplace. In addition to brand-name items, ships now include the same outlets that are found at many ports of call. Norwegian Cruise Line's newest ships, for example, include a Colombian Emeralds International store.

Shipboard shops have also become more competitively priced. At one time they tended to offer the same items found at ports, but at higher prices. Today the ship's shops compete aggressively with land-based outlets. Almost all shipboard shops run promotions, such as "gold by the inch" or "designer watches," to bring passengers into their stores and to increase sales.

Some shipboard shops guarantee their prices by offering to meet the price of any comparable item bought ashore, or to refund the difference between their price and the onshore price. The offer is, however, somewhat empty. You have to actually buy the item ashore and bring the receipt onboard — which means you'd be stuck with two identical watches or two identical necklaces. While the offer gives the impression of competitive pricing, the guarantee has little value.

We Know You'll Want a Photo of Yourself

"I'm not making any money on this cruise. I had to pay the concessionaire to be here, I have to pay for my film and supplies, I'm taking lots of pictures, but I'm not selling enough to even break even."

That is what I was told by a photographer on a two-week ultra-luxury cruise. Like most ship photographers, she worked under a subcontract with the concessionaire that provided photographers to the cruise line. (Carnival Cruise Line and Princess Cruises are exceptions in that they keep their photographic services in-house.) In addition to taking photographs throughout the cruise — beginning with when you embark and ending the second to last night of the cruise — the photographic outlet sells film and batteries for cameras and provides photofinishing. Some also sell cameras at duty-free prices.

Shipboard photographers miss few opportunities to take pictures. Passengers pose with the captain as they enter the Captain's Welcome Cocktail Party, have their picture taken at dinner on formal nights and on theme nights, and can choose from several occasions to have a formal portrait done. As well, many candid shots are snapped as passengers leave the ship at a port of call, while on shore excursions or tours, and as they go about their day onboard. All photos are on display to make purchases easy.

People tend to want vacation photographs of themselves, so sales are practically guaranteed. Photographers further encourage sales by offering discounts for multiple pictures or by providing an added value to the photo, such as a photo album or frame. One operator increased net photo revenue on a single ship by $1 million a year through offering passengers a discounted price and a souvenir photo album for pre-purchasing six photos. Passengers were offered a package deal that included five photos (price: $7 each), an 8 x 10 portrait (price: $12), and a souvenir album (price: $20) — a $67 value for $40. The scheme increased net revenue by $1.39 per passenger, per day.[14]

(The contrast between his success and the experience of the insolvent photographer mentioned earlier is due mainly to the difference in buying habits of passengers onboard mass market and ultraluxury cruise ships; the latter purchase few photographs.)

"Attract passengers with good pricing and merchandising. Entertain them at all costs. Fill them up. Strip them clean. Send them home happy."[15]

— J. Norman Howard, former business director, Cunard Line

Open Your Wallet and We'll Show You the Sights

In December 2001 I visited St. John in the US Virgin Islands. My partner and I took a taxi to Trunk Bay. The trip cost us $6 each way, $12 total including a tip. The cruise ship offered the identical trip, in identical taxis, for $43 per person.

The sale of ship-sponsored shore excursions is a significant source of revenue. Depending on the port, between 50 and 80 percent of passengers purchase a shore excursion. Three companies — International Voyager Media, Onboard Media, and the PPI Group — operate the vast majority of shore excursion programs.

The shore excursion provided by the cruise line is convenient — but the cost for this convenience is considerable. The shore excursion concessionaire contracts with a local tour operator, then offers the program to the cruise line. Each one adds to the price. The markups create resentment among passengers who expect more than what they receive. For a shore excursion that costs the passenger $60, the local tour operator receives between $15 and $20. The passenger expects to receive a product worth $60, but the operator receives nowhere near this amount for the tour provided.

My Script Says These Are the Things to See

Closely allied with the sale of shore excursions are "port lectures," spiels about the port's attractions, including shopping, as part of the sightseeing tour. The same company contracted to provide shore excursions often provides the port lecturer. The lecturer's income may be tied to the number of shore excursions purchased by passengers, in the form of a bonus for generated sales.

Although port lecturers tell passengers about the sights in a port, rarely are they hired for their expertise on either the port or travel in general. Port lecturers are given a script to read and they tend to follow it fairly closely. When they deviate, the information provided can be amazingly incorrect.

A main focus of the port lecturer's job is to talk about shopping. He or she gives cruise ship passengers a map which identifies "approved" stores, explaining that the main advantage of shopping at these stores is that the quality and value of merchandise is guaranteed, and the cruise line will facilitate refunds if the purchased product is not as it was advertised and sold. They are clear that refunds cannot be had in a case of buyer regret, but getting a refund for other reasons is often more difficult than you are led to believe. Only a few cruise lines will tell you that the stores on the approved list have paid a fee to be included.

A 1999 article in the *Boston Globe* cites a gem and jewelry specialist who warns that jewelry fraud is rampant abroad. She described cruise ship passengers as "lambs being herded to slaughter." According to this specialist: "These stores are taking advantage of the fact that people are looking for bargains.... Everyone wants a memento of their trip and, for women, jewelry is one of the favorite mementos."[16] As for the cruise line's guarantee, she points out that it is an easy promise to make since most people don't bother to check anything out when they get home. Those who do bother often find that getting a refund is not easy.

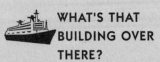

WHAT'S THAT BUILDING OVER THERE?

During a cruise on Norwegian Cruise Line's *Norwegian Crown*, we were sailing in France down the Seine River from Le Havre to Rouen. Along the way the port lecturer provided a commentary, at one point telling passengers: "And to our right is a small French village named Gendarmerie." She had assumed the sign over an administrative-looking building bore the village's name; actually, it identified the police station.

GETTING A REFUND IS NOT AS EASY AS THEY SAY

The most common dispute over port purchases relates to the value of jewelry. Passengers are often "guaranteed" that the item is better priced than it would be at home. While most accept this claim without question, some buyers have unhappily discovered that it was unfounded. Consider the following:

- The *Condé Nast Traveler* ombudsman reported in 1996 a case where a passenger on Carnival Cruise Line's *Sensation*, during a shore excursion at Ocho Rios, Jamaica, purchased a diamond engagement ring at Colours for $2,350. An appraisal certificate for $4,450 accompanied the ring. When the passenger returned home, he took the ring for an independent appraisal and was told it was worth $600 less than what he had paid. The passenger followed the refund application instructions he had been given on the ship, but to no avail. The store refused to accept the credentials of the passenger's independent jeweler, and Carnival stood behind the store's position. Not until the passenger secured the *Condé Nast Traveler* ombudsman's assistance was a refund finally provided.[17]

- The "Consumer Beat" column in the *Boston Globe* reported on a similar case in 1999. A cruise ship passenger had purchased a tanzanite and diamond ring at Rachat & Romero in Cozumel, Mexico, while traveling with Celebrity Cruises. He had paid $2,400 for a ring that the Mexican jeweler appraised at $6,530. After the passenger returned home, he sought an independent appraisal and was told the ring's value was $1,900. When he approached Rachat & Romero, they said their appraised price was more like a suggested retail price, even though it was identified on a document entitled "certified appraisal." Although the *Boston Globe* was able to secure a refund offer, the passenger rejected it, on the basis that to agree "to a refund would be letting the cruise line and jeweler off too easily." He said, "They're basically saying you caught us at fraud so what we'll do is give you your money back. I think that stinks. How many other people are they ripping off?"[18]

Get Your Hair Done for That Formal Night

Cruise ships traditionally offer personal services such as hairstyling, manicures, pedicures, facials, and massages. Over the past decade the range of services has expanded with introduction of larger and more elaborate spas. Increasingly, the full range of personal indulgences available at a spa at home is available at sea.[19] Prices at sea are no less than at home; in fact, they are often much higher.[20]

A concessionaire provides the spa and personal services. A British-based company called Steiner Leisure Limited has almost exclusive control over spa services provided to the cruise industry. In 2001 the company had the concession for 23 cruise lines, including more than 100 ships.

One of Steiner's competitors was Mandara Spa on Star Cruises and Norwegian Cruise Line. Mandara had contracted with Norwegian Cruise Line in 2000 after the cruise line chose not to renew with Steiner. Ironically, Steiner acquired Mandara Spa in June 2001.[22]

 **DEEP CLEANING**

Every week Steiner Leisure employees at sea massage more than 30,000 bodies, deep-cleanse 15,000 faces, blow-dry 6,000 heads of hair, and manicure approximately 6,000 pairs of hands.[21]

Scheduled for completion in December 2003, the spa on the *Queen Mary 2* will be designed and operated by a newcomer to the cruise industry: Canyon Ranch Health Resorts. Canyon Ranch has two of its own ships under construction.

New and Better Ideas for Separating You from Your Money

Cruise lines continue to introduce more ways to grab a passenger's money. The late 1990s introduced the onboard art auction, which quickly became one of the most lucrative endeavors. Indeed, on some cruises this is the single largest source of onboard revenue.

Fine Art at Kmart Prices

You can now purchase fine art while on your cruise. I have been given a chance to buy art by Rodin, Dali, Picasso, Chagall, Erte, and others of comparable stature — amazing the deals that can be had on art by a 20th-century master, and all available at onboard art auctions!

Norwegian Cruise Line introduced shipboard art auctions in the mid-1990s. Once other cruise lines realized the income potential, they quickly followed suit. On most cruise lines, auctions are handled by one of two companies — the same contractors that handle most shore excursions. Onboard Media (owned by Louis Vuitton Moët Hennessy), through its sister company Cruise Management International (which has a partnership with Park West Gallery), serves Celebrity Cruises, Costa Cruises, Carnival Cruise Line, Crystal Cruises, Holland America Line, Princess Cruises, and Royal Caribbean International. The PPI Group, publisher of *Porthole* magazine, is the other major player.

Two strategies are commonly used to attract passengers to the auctions. One is to provide free champagne to anyone previewing the art and/or attending the auction. The other is to have the auction include art, often signed serigraphs or lithographs, of well-known artists.

The main selling point used by auctioneers is that pieces of art may be had for as much as 80 percent off shoreside prices. Many passengers report that this claim is accurate, although a February 2001 article in *USA Today* cites a number of people who dispute its accuracy. In one case, the same piece of art bought on the ship was found at the neighborhood Kmart for sale at a fraction of the shipboard auction price. No matter which view is correct, art auctions are big business. Park West Gallery reported selling 200,000 pieces of art aboard cruise ships in the year 2000.[23]

The cruise passenger who buys art at an onboard auction has some surprises ahead. In most cases, the auction house adds a charge of 10 to 15 percent to the winning bid — a charge that is added only after the auction is over. Granted, that's standard practice at onshore auction houses, but in my experience, cruise ship passengers aren't made aware of the surcharge until they go to pay for their purchases. As well, because the art is shipped from the company's warehouse in the United States, expect to pay additional charges for shipping and handling. Art that seems to be a bargain can quickly exceed the expected price.

The unsophisticated buyer is also taken advantage of in other ways. Because the numbered piece being bid on is not the same piece that the buyer will receive, its actual value may be different. A serigraph numbered 3 of 300 has a different value to a collector than one numbered 298 of 300. In addition, cruise passengers tend to believe the advice and appraisal of the auctioneer. As suggested by Stephen Abt, CEO of ArtFact Inc., "You should never get your market information from someone who's selling art."[24]

Despite the hype, you may not find bargain artwork on a cruise ship. Regardless, most passengers are unable to resist the temptation to purchase art by a recognizable name, or in the face of being told that the piece they are being offered is a steal. Remember the old saying: If something seems too good to be true, it probably is.

Table 2.1

PER CAPITA REVENUE FROM ONBOARD SPENDING, HOLLAND AMERICA LINE, 1996-2001

REVENUE SOURCE	INCREASE OVER 5-YEAR PERIOD
Bar Sales	18%
Casino	22%
Miscellaneous*	60%
Photography	30%
Retail Sales	38%
Shore Excursions	73%
Spa Services	53%
Overall Average	41%

Source: Mark Barnard (Manager, On-Board Revenue; Holland America Line - Westours, Inc.), PowerPoint presentation given at trade show, Session 9: "Maximizing On-Board Revenue and the Benefits of I.T.," Seatrade Cruise Shipping Convention (Miami, FL), March 14, 2002.

* This category includes communication charges, art auctions, bingo, gift orders, Internet use, and onboard promotions.

Our Private Island — Designed for Your Enjoyment

Private islands are another way that cruise lines generate income. In the early 1990s Norwegian Cruise Line was the first to introduce the concept. The innovation provided an alternative to landing passengers in already congested ports. It could also serve as a port of call on Sundays to eliminate passenger complaints about shoreside shops being closed.

For cruise lines, the private island has several economic benefits. For one, passengers on a private island are a captive market. The cruise line runs all beverage sales and concessions such as tours, water activities, souvenirs, and convenience shops. There is no competition so all money spent on the island contributes to its revenue and profit, and as an added benefit, passengers tend to enjoy the experience. This provides both a positive impression of the cruise line and an indirect source of future revenue in the form of passenger referrals.[25]

Private islands also contribute to the economic bottom line of the cruise line because of their location. Most are in the Bahamas or Haiti. With a stop at the private island, ships are able to save fuel by cruising at a slower speed between two primary ports. Rather than sailing nonstop from St. Thomas to Miami, for example, a ship may reduce speed between the two ports with its scheduled stop at the private island. The ship saves money and at the same time increases passenger satisfaction.

If You Have Any Money Left …

While most people go on a cruise to relax, many of them also want to participate in a range of activities. Cruise ships of the 1980s provided many activities, and most were offered at no cost. Cruise ships today have increased the choice of activities, but many come with a fee.

Bingo is a traditional activity on cruise ships. As recently as the mid-1990s, you could purchase cards for the four or five games in a bingo session for $5. Now, the cost of playing has increased to $25 or $35 for an equivalent set of bingo cards. The size of the jackpot has increased accordingly. Combined with promotions such as offering a free cruise to the winner of a particular game, bigger jackpots serve to increase the level of participation.

Bingo games, like spa treatments, are used for cross-promotions, a chance to advertise other products and revenue-generating activities.[26]

Innovations and new activities for children include video games and virtual reality centers, rock-climbing walls, computers, child-only shore excursions, and ice-skating rinks. Adults may be attracted to golf simulators ($20 an hour) or to culinary workshops ($395 a session). The price for activities varies from ship to ship; cruise lines tend to change with what the market will bear. No matter what the charge, those fun activities quickly contribute to the overall cost of your supposedly all-inclusive vacation.

Come to Our Outdoor Steakhouse

One of the newest waves on cruise ships is the provision of alternative dining rooms. While attractive in that they offer a change from the main restaurant, alternative dining rooms come with a cost. This starkly contrasts with the idea that cruise fares include all meals.

Carnival Cruise Lines unveiled its alternative supper club in 2001 with a $20 surcharge, a year later raised to $25. Celebrity Cruises introduced its alternative dining in 2001 under the banner of Michel Roux cuisine and charged $25. Portofino's, a dining room on Royal Caribbean International's *Radiance of the Seas*, charges $26. In comparison, Princess Cruises' alternative restaurants are a relative bargain. Two restaurants charge a reservation fee of $3.50, purportedly to prevent people from not showing for the reserved time. In 2001 Princess introduced an outdoor steakhouse with an $8 charge.

One of Norwegian Cruise Line's newest ships, the *Norwegian Star*, boasts ten separate restaurants; the cost associated with each dining option is not explicitly advertised. While the traditional dining option is free of cost, several of the alternatives have a $10 cover charge. A couple of other restaurants are a la carte with appetizers and entrees, including lobster, fish, and steak, at market prices.

In addition to charging for alternative restaurants, many ships now charge for snacks and other items. Initially, the charges were only for specialty items such as Häagen Dazs ice cream: on Princess

Cruises $1.90 for a scoop, $3.50 for a sundae. Other cruise lines quickly followed suit with charges for gourmet coffees and cappuccino. Today, a passenger is likely to pay extra for pastries, cookies, and chocolates offered through café-style food outlets.

The logic of extra charges for food is sometimes difficult to grasp. On Celebrity Cruises, for example, you can order a glass of orange juice from room service at no charge. However, if you order a glass of orange juice at one of the bars, it costs $2.00. The same glass of orange juice ordered in the dining room when it is not the "juice of the night" costs $1.50.

Keep in Touch with Loved Ones Back Home

Cruise ships have always offered telephone service. But before you pick up the phone in your room and make a call, you might want to know that the price for telephone calls ranges from $4 to $15 a minute, depending on the cruise line. As with other income generators, all too often you don't discover the cost until the end of the cruise.

The growth of the Internet has led many ships to install cyber cafés. A concessionaire provides these services; the largest is Digital Seas. Again, the cost varies from ship to ship, usually ranging from $0.75 to $1.50 per minute, with a minimum charge of 10 or 15 minutes. Crystal Cruises charges an initial set-up fee of $5.00 and $3.00 for each e-mail message sent. Like other money grabs, income is sufficient for both the concessionaire and the cruise line to recover costs and make a profit. Although this is unsurprising practice for a business, it is surprising to the cruise passenger who was expecting an "all-inclusive" vacation.

We Can Make Money Even When You're in Your Cabin

In the mid- to late 1990s cruise lines began to introduce revenue-generating schemes in passenger cabins. They realized there was money to be made while passengers were in their room relaxing, preparing for dinner, or simply lazing away time in bed.

The earliest innovation was interactive multimedia. You can preview shore excursion options and reserve your choices, order wine for dinner from the ship's wine list, order pay-per-view movies (including X-rated films on some cruise lines), play video poker and similar games, and in some cases even shop. The advent of interactive television transforms traditional shipboard revenue downtime into revenue-generating time.

In the late 1990s minibars began appearing in passenger cabins, offering soft drinks, wine, liquor, and snack foods.[27] Disney Cruise Line, among the first to introduce in-cabin minibars, had one type with a clear glass front. As the manufacturer stated, this would allow passengers to see all the snack items inside, thus precipitating the impulse buy — particularly effective when children are staying in the cabin.[28]

As in many hotels, minibars on cruise ships are beginning to use a system employing infrared light that automatically logs an item as purchased when it is picked up or removed; the charge immediately appears on a passenger's shipboard account. The system is attractive to the cruise line because it eliminates the need for staff to check what has been consumed. However, until passengers become accustomed to these systems, there will be many erroneous charges. If you take an item out and then return it unused, the charge is not reversed. Because of passenger complaints, Royal Caribbean has removed minibars with these systems.

Internet access in passenger cabins is the newest wave for capturing additional income. Many new ships are being built with fiber-optic networks to all cabins, and networks are being installed on some older ships.

MORE WAYS TO IMPROVE THE BOTTOM LINE

In addition to encouraging onboard spending, a company can improve its economic bottom line in two basic ways.

One is to reduce costs. Cruise ships have done this effectively by cutting back on whatever can be eliminated or reduced, particularly amenities (e.g., shampoo, soaps, and other such bathroom items) and "freebies" (e.g., playing cards, pens and notepads, chocolates placed on your pillow at night) that were common as recently as a few years ago. They have also introduced cost-saving systems, such as the SeaSupplier e-procurement system adopted by Royal Caribbean Cruises which is expected to save from 15 to 20 percent of total purchasing expenses — as much as $120 million per year. And consolidation in the industry produces economies of scale and increased purchasing power.

Both Royal Caribbean Cruises and Carnival Corporation projected in early 2002 that a merger with P&O Princess would save $100 million per year.

The other way to improve the bottom line is, obviously, to increase revenue. Onboard revenue is not the only means of doing so.

Port Charges

There was a time when cruise lines earned substantial income through "port charges," fees added to the advertised cruise fare when you made your reservation, but a class-action lawsuit in 1996 changed all that.[29] Most cruise companies agreed to stop stating additional charges in small print at the bottom of the page or the back of a brochure. Instead, industry practice became to advertise cruises with port charges and all other fees included in the promoted price.

Resolution of that 1996 lawsuit also changed the way port charges are computed. Some previously included items were eliminated, but it's still hard to figure out exactly what is included. Holland America Line's general counsel suggested there are a lot of costs incurred when a ship is in port and these are included as port charges. These include not just taxes and fees, but pilot and tugboat services, stevedoring, and garbage hauling. Like others, Holland America Line refused to identify all expenses under port charges, arguing that such information could undermine its competitive advantage.

One estimate during the lawsuit was that as much as 50 percent of the total amount collected as port charges was used to cover overhead rather than what was needed to pay the fees charged by ports of call. The total overcharge was estimated to be $600 million and involved seven companies: Royal Caribbean Cruise Line, Celebrity Cruises, Norwegian Cruise Line, Princess Cruises, Carnival Cruise Line, Holland America Line, and Renaissance Cruises.[30]

We'll Reward You for Bringing Passengers

As a result of recent events, a new wrinkle surrounds port fees. Following the World Trade Center attack in September 2001, many cruise lines redeployed their ships from Europe and Asia to itineraries closer to the United States. Hoping to capitalize on this shift, Cartagena, Colombia, quickly offered a 50-percent reduction in its port charges for any ship adding a stop at its port. San Juan, Puerto Rico, reduced its port charges by 25 percent.

A year earlier Panama had introduced an innovative scheme to attract cruise ship business. It offered a bounty for each cruise passenger landed at a Panamanian port. The per-person payment ranged from $2.50 to $12.00, the amount increasing with the number of landed passengers. The bounty had the desired effect of attracting cruise ships to Panama's ports. For some ships, traditional seven-day itineraries weren't long enough to travel the necessary distance; Carnival Cruise Line introduced an eight-day itinerary in order to take advantage of the bounty offer.

The beauty of Panama's scheme, from the cruise line's perspective, is that the amount of port charges assessed to passengers is not reduced. And, at the same time, the cruise line receives a direct payment from the port of call. The scenario is something like this: each passenger pays the cruise line $10 to cover port charges (which in turn covers expenses) and the cruise line is then paid the $12 bounty for bringing in the passenger (pure profit). Not a bad arrangement for the company.

No other ports have yet followed Panama's example, but the scheme just began in 2001. It is initially scheduled to run for five years. Whether Panama's success encourages other ports to initiate similar incentives remains to be seen.

Port Facilities as a Profit Source

Another mechanism for generating income is a trend toward cruise lines trying to take a portion of income generated at a particular port by building new or improving existing port facilities, and at the same time being given economic incentives for the construction or improvements. The first arrangement of this sort was announced in August 2001 following two years of negotiation between the Florida-Caribbean Cruise Association and the US Virgin Islands. The negotiations followed a March 1999 announcement by Virgin Islands officials that they planned to immediately hike the head tax by 33 percent to $9.50 per passenger. In response to opposition from St. Thomas merchants and from cruise lines, the hike was canceled and alternatives explored.

The agreement reached in August 2001 provided for increases in the number of cruise line passengers brought to the US Virgin Islands during the off-season between May and September — over five years, a 15-percent annual increase on St. Croix and a 10-percent annual increase on St. Thomas. It also provided for Carnival Corporation and Royal Caribbean Cruise Ltd to jointly develop port facilities at St. Thomas's Crown Bay.[31]

Under the agreement, the two companies agreed to invest $31 million to enlarge the two-berth pier so it could accommodate each cruise line's newest mega-ships. They also agreed to improve 7.5 acres of adjacent land into an area offering taxis and tour dispatch, and to include 90,000 square feet of retail, restaurant, and amphitheater space. Five thousand square feet would be reserved for local vendors and would include a theme attraction based on the islands' sugar cane heritage, a rum distillery, and a terminal to accommodate homeporting of smaller ships.[32]

In return for their investment, Carnival and Royal Caribbean would enjoy priority berthing for a 30-year period and retain 75 percent of the head tax charged passengers.[33] In addition, the terms of the lease of the land provided for the cruise lines to receive a percentage of revenue from retail operations. Passengers, through port charges, would provide the investment needed for the project; the cruise lines would enjoy the profits.

Six months after the project was announced, the governor of the US Virgin Islands canceled the letter of intent, saying he believed that "it is important that the V.I. maintain full control of its harbor and harbor development."[34] The governor's announcement followed considerable public discussion about the positive value of local investment and local control over Crown Bay. There were also indications that the deal would not be approved by the Virgin Island's Senate. Less than two month's after the letter of intent was canceled, Carnival Cruise Line stopped all port calls at St. Croix. Carnival's stated reason for the decision had to do with the value of the island to passengers and with concerns for passenger safety, given a number of recent muggings on the island.

Also in August 2001 Carnival Corporation announced that it would invest $8.5 million to upgrade Pier Four at San Juan, Puerto Rico. This would make it practical for the huge 3,400-passenger, 102,000-ton Destiny-class vessels to be homeported at San Juan. In return for the investment, Carnival Corporation enjoys preferential berthing at the pier for a period of 20 years. It will recoup its investment by retaining a portion of the port charges paid by passengers.

In November 2001 Carnival Corporation announced an agreement with the Port of Cancun, Mexico, to invest more than $40 million in a homeport/transit port facility at Xcaret. The project, built on 21 acres of land, is a joint venture with Parque Xcaret, a local Mexican company. What benefits or incentives were provided to Carnival Corporation is unclear, but it was indicated that the facility is a private port under a government concession and not obligated to accommodate other cruise lines. For Carnival, perhaps the greatest value of the new port is that it makes practical a range of new itineraries, including mini-cruise alternatives to the traditional Bahamas-Key West routes from ports in Florida.[35]

THE NON-ALL-INCLUSIVE VACATION

As you see, a cruise is anything but all-inclusive. How much more your vacation costs varies widely from person to person, but it is difficult to get by with no additional expenses. Some cruise lines have begun automatically charging passenger shipboard accounts for gratuities (in amounts set by the cruise line); this practice is discussed further in Chapter 5. While the initial price of a cruise may be reasonable, the extras can quickly add up.

BEYOND THE MUSTER DRILL

I HAVE TAKEN 30 CRUISES since 1992. I have been in Belize City with temperatures well over 100 degrees and returned to a ship with no air conditioning. I have spent two days on a ship "dead in the water" at the mouth of the Rio de Plata during a spring storm that closed the harbor at Buenos Aires, before finally being given permission to dock at Montevideo because of a "humanitarian emergency" — the ship had no running water for almost two days. I have been on a ship that encountered 50-foot seas and gale-force-nine winds, forcing it to abandon efforts to reach the Beagle Channel at the southern tip of South America. And I have twice been adrift on ships that had no propulsion and limited electrical power. Each of these experiences was an adventure. I have, fortunately, been spared anything more serious.

Most people go on a cruise expecting to be pampered and to have a carefree, trouble-free vacation. Advertising and pre-cruise information provided by the cruise line support these expectations. Passengers may be warned about risks when going ashore, but nothing is said about the risks aboard the ship. And there are risks — although, granted, relatively small — that passengers should know about.

A common problem over the past couple of years has been canceled cruises due to late delivery of new ships: for example, Holland America Line's *Rotterdam, Volendam,* and *Zaandam*; Radisson Seven Seas Cruises' *Paul Gauguin*; Disney Cruise Line's *Disney Magic*; Princess Cruises' *Grand Princess* and *Sea Princess*; Carnival Cruise Lines' *Triumph*; Celebrity Cruises' *Millennium*; and Royal Olympic Cruises' *Olympic Explorer*. In fact, late deliveries became so customary that people were booking maiden

49

voyages with hopes that the cruise would be canceled and they would receive a free cruise as compensation for the inconvenience!

By 2001, however, cruise lines learned and allowed additional time to cover any event of late delivery, thereby avoiding the need to cancel cruises. In the case of Holland America Line's *Zuiderdam*, the company went so far as to announce an entire year in advance that the ship's delivery in late 2002 would be delayed by 45 days.

Ships pulled from service because of mechanical problems present a similar inconvenience. This often occurs with newer ships that use recent technology and have defects in materials or machinery. There have been a number of problems with azimuthing podded propulsion systems. Carnival Cruise Line's *Paradise* and *Elation* both underwent unscheduled maintenance in 2000 because of problems with their Azipod propulsion systems. Celebrity Cruises' *Millennium* and *Infinity* similarly had multiple cruises canceled — the Millennium in 2000 and again in 2001, the *Infinity* in 2001 — because of problems with their Mermaid propulsion systems. In May 2002 Celebrity Cruises' *Constellation* had its first sailing canceled after problems with one of its podded propulsion units were discovered during sea trials.

> In the 20 years following the fire onboard the Angelina Lauro, which sunk in the US Virgin Islands in March 1979, "the Safety Board has investigated 25 major accidents involving foreign cruise ships operating from US ports. Of those 25 accidents, 16 involved fires. As a result of those fire-involved accidents, there were 8 fatalities, 210 personal injuries, and over $175 million in property damage."
>
> — Jim Hall, US National Transportation Safety Board, October 7, 1999

SHIP SAFETY

More serious than cancellations and delays are mishaps at sea. Although uncommon, mishaps are still frequent enough that passengers should be aware of the chance that things can and at times will go wrong. Unsurprisingly, the cruise industry prefers that passengers not have this knowledge. They see their product as competing with land-based resorts (hotels and the like), which, unlike cruise ships, don't run aground, don't collide with anything, and much less frequently have disabling fires.

Fender Benders, Failures, and Fires, Oh My!

Like other modes of transportation, traveling by sea has risks. There have been numerous incidents involving mechanical failure, fires,[2] ships running aground,[3] and collisions, as well as the odd occasion of sinking ships that are abandoned at sea. In most cases, the mishaps are relatively minor and attributed to human error.

Between January 2000 and December 2001, more than 70 cruise ship mishaps were reported in the media, including engine failures with the ship adrift for as long as 27 hours (often without functioning plumbing or air conditioning), disabling fires resulting in loss of electricity and propulsion, and several ships running aground (see Appendix 1). The *Costa Tropicale* actually ran aground twice within two weeks: the first time, in Venice, it was freed by tugboats; the second time it required the assistance of its sister ship, the *Costa Atlantica*, after several unsuccessful rescue efforts by tugboats.

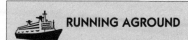

RUNNING AGROUND

According to the US Coast Guard, a total of 20 cruise ships ran aground in Alaska's coastal waters in the three-year period from August 1996 to August 1999.

Who's Watching Where We're Going?

Cruise ship mishaps can be more serious than engine failures and being left adrift. You may recall the early morning collision in the English Channel in 1999 when Norwegian Cruise Line's *Norwegian Dream* collided with the freighter *Ever Decent*. Pictures appeared in most newspapers showing cargo containers on the front deck of the *Norwegian Dream*'s mauled bow. Miraculously, there were no serious injuries, particularly given the dangerous cargo, including toxic chemicals, carried by the *Ever Decent*.

Other major collisions involving cruise ships include:

- the 1989 collision of Carnival Cruise Line's *Celebration* with a Cuban cement freighter, resulting in three deaths on the freighter[4]
- a 1991 collision involving the *Island Princess* and the *Regent Sea*, causing major damage to both ships, while they were in port at Skagway, Alaska

- the 1992 collision between the *Europa* and a freighter 180 miles off the Hong Kong coast
- the 1992 collision of the *Royal Pacific* with a fishing vessel, resulting in both ships sinking and the deaths of approximately 100 people
- the 1993 collision of the *Noordam* with a freighter in the Gulf of Mexico.[5]

There have also been serious near misses. In 1997 Carnival Cruise Line's *Jubilee* barely avoided a middle-of-the-night collision with a fishing vessel off the California coast.[6] A year earlier Holland America Line's *Statendam* narrowly missed colliding with a barge carrying 21,000 gallons of propane and palettes of dynamite in the Discovery Passage, British Columbia.[7]

Ships Do Sink

In addition to the *Royal Pacific* sinking in 1992, other cruise ships have sunk. In 1998 Windjammer Cruises' flagship, *Fantome*, sunk as it attempted to avoid Hurricane Mitch. There were no passengers aboard but 30 crew members died. In December 1999 Premier Cruises' *Seabreeze* sank in high seas off the east coast of the United States. No passengers were aboard and all seafarers were rescued.

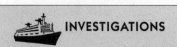 **INVESTIGATIONS**

Between 1980 and 1992 the US Coast Guard investigated 73 accidents involving large cruise ships. These included 13 collisions, 16 fires, 22 equipment or material failures, and 22 groundings.

Other ships that have gone down in recent years include: the *Sir Francis Drake*, which sunk in 1999 while moored during a hurricane; the *Sun Vista* (previously Celebrity Cruises' *Meridian*), which also in 1999 sunk off Malaysia following an engine room fire that could not be contained; New Paradise Cruises' *Romantica*, which sunk in the Mediterranean in 1997 after an engine room fire;[8] and Starlauro's *Achille Lauro*, which went down in the Indian Ocean off the Seychelles in 1994. Only in the sinking of the *Achille Lauro* was there any loss of life: four people died and eight were injured.

Interestingly, Holland America Line's new *Prinsendam* — previously sailing as the *Seabourn Sun* and before that as the *Royal Viking Sun* — is named after a vessel which in 1980 sunk 140 miles off the coast of Alaska following an engine room fire that necessitated a middle-of-the-night abandoning of the ship.

Who's Responsible for Cruise Ship Safety?

In May 2001 Norwegian Cruise Line's *Norway* was detained in Miami following a US Coast Guard inspection that found 106 leaks in the ship's fire sprinkler system. The leaks had been temporarily patched with soft rubber, which "a fire could melt ... and the compromised pipe's loss of pressure would threaten the entire

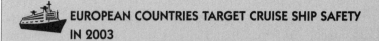 **EUROPEAN COUNTRIES TARGET CRUISE SHIP SAFETY IN 2003**

Under the July 2001 Paris Memorandum of Understanding on Port State Control (Paris MOU), European countries will target cruise ships in a concentrated inspection campaign beginning in May 2003.[13] The 2001 Paris MOU grew out of concerns about operational standards on passenger vessels following the release of inspection data for 2000, which indicated an 80-percent increase in operational deficiencies — including inadequate firefighting and safety equipment — over the previous four years.

The Paris MOU cited the human element as the weak link in onboard safety and emphasized that it should remain a focus of attention for port state control. Richard Schiferli, secretary of the Paris MOU, suggested that many ship owners did not pay enough attention to the interaction between "hardware" and "software"; that is, between the physical facility (the ship itself) and the workers (hired to supposedly make things run smoothly and safely).

The Paris MOU was issued after a high profile incident in which a cruise ship, *Ocean Glory I*, was detained in Dover after the British Maritime and Coastguard Agency discovered 35 deficiencies and refused permission for the ship to sail. Built in 1950, the *Ocean Glory I* was flagged in Panama and operated by Greece-based Cruise Holdings, which had the ship on long-term charter from Mediterranean Shipping Cruises. Following this incident the ship was retired rather than repaired.[14]

sprinkler system."[9] A passenger report led to the investigation; the situation had been overlooked in the ship's semi-annual inspection just three months earlier.[10]

All ships visiting American ports undergo Coast Guard inspections, and generally, serious safety problems are found. With ships that do not visit American ports, safety is left up to the cruise line. Unfortunately, safety is taken less seriously than many of us might like. The Paris Memorandum of Understanding on Port State Control (Paris MOU) is one of several regional agreements the world over between countries sharing common waters (in this case, the North Atlantic and Europe); its focus is on harmonized inspection regimes of ships to ensure compliance with international rules on safety, pollution prevention, and the living and working conditions of crew. In July 2001 Canada and the 18 European countries then party to the agreement identified cruise ship safety as a major problem, but a delay of almost two years precedes any concerted effort to deal with it.[11] Like the recent inquiry into ship safety by the International Commission on Shipping (ICONS) — the final report subtitled *Ships, Slaves and Competition*[12] — the participating governments acknowledge human error as the principal cause of shipping accidents and pollution incidents.

There are two elements to the human factor. The most serious problem, identified by both ICONS and the International Transport Workers' Federation (ITF) — a worldwide federation of transport workers' trade unions that represents the interests of shipboard employees — is worker fatigue. Many of the people responsible for navigation of the ship simply fail to receive enough rest.

In its study entitled *Seafarer Fatigue: Wake Up to the Dangers*, based on a survey of 2,500 seafarers representing 60 nationalities and 63 flags of registration, the ITF reports two cases of officers on watch dozing off while supposedly in control of fast ferries; and one case of a grounding that occurred after deck officers had been working an average of 16 hours a day, with no opportunity for sleep longer than 3 hours. One respondent, a first officer on a cruise ship, reported that on his previous ship he had worked 12- to 15-hour days, never had 6 hours of continuous sleep, and had worked 87 hours a week for three months straight. He said he regularly made errors in passage planning and execution, and that he dared not sit down while on watch.[15] The problem of cruise line employee fatigue is addressed in greater detail in Chapter 5.

The second major problem is that cruise lines do not always follow their own operational guidelines. Investigators into the 1999 collision between the *Norwegian Dream* and the *Ever Decent* found that although NCL company policy required two officers to be on watch, only one officer was on the bridge prior to the collision. In addition, the report issued by the government of the Bahamas (the country of registry for the *Norwegian Dream*) said the single officer on watch became confused immediately before the collision, and in several areas his bridge practice fell short of the ideal. While he relied heavily on the use of radar for his anti-collision work, he did few visual checks and did not make the most effective use of the radar data provided. As well, he appeared to ignore warnings of the impending collision and he was distracted by a series of clerical tasks that were his responsibility in addition to his being the only officer on the bridge.[16] It is hard to know whether the collision would have been averted had company policy been followed.

SHIP SECURITY — THE THIN VENEER OF FEELING SAFE

Aside from safety of the ship itself, there is the issue of the security of those onboard. Security involves a number of different facets, including, for one, fire safety. The National Transportation Safety Board (NTSB) has raised the issue many times during the 1990s.

Following a 1991 fire on Royal Caribbean Cruise Line's *Sovereign of the Seas*,[17] the NTSB was able to effect several new safety features. However, it has not always been that successful. Its concerns about the chimney-effect presented by atriums on new cruise ships were ignored. In 1996 a fire on the *Universe Explorer* caused the deaths of 5 crew members and injuries to 67 crew and 3 passengers.[18] Two fires the following year aboard the *Vistafjord* resulted in no injuries in the first incident but one crew member died and six passengers and nine crew suffered minor injuries in the second fire.[19] Following those events, the NTSB called for fire and smoke alarms that sounded in passenger cabins rather than only on the bridge. The industry response was negative.

Five years later, in 2001, the cruise industry finally conceded and agreed to install local-sounding smoke detectors and fire alarms in passenger cabins. Considerable media attention was given to that commitment, made by the industry's lobbyist and political spokesperson, the International Council of Cruise Lines (ICCL); however, the ICCL made no commitment as to when its promise would be fulfilled.

Among the various security issues, foremost to many people is personal safety.

Feel Secure: We Check Photo IDs of Everyone Coming Onboard

Following the events of September 11, 2001, considerable attention has been given to shipboard security. The cruise industry first confronted this issue following the hijacking by terrorists of the *Achille Lauro* in 1985. A year later, the International Maritime Organization (IMO) adopted a set of voluntary guidelines, published under the title *Measures to Prevent Unlawful Acts Against Passengers and Crews On Board Ships.*

In 1987 the US Coast Guard put forth its own Voluntary Guidelines for Cruise Ship and Terminal Security, patterned after the IMO measures. By 1994 the Coast Guard had concluded that many security measures were being ignored or only partially implemented. It therefore announced plans for a set of mandatory security regulations for passenger vessels and passenger terminals.

The Coast Guard believed that cruise ships and cruise lines should maintain the highest level of security at all times and asserted that, despite the expenses associated with its proposal, the benefits would far outweigh the costs. The cruise industry opposed the guidelines on the basis that they were "too stringent and inflexible" and voiced its concerns to the American government.

Industry opposition led to a revised set of rules, implemented in 1996. The Coast Guard introduced a three-level security system, based on assessment of the risk level. At the lowest level were nine mandatory standard measures for all cruise ships homeported or calling at ports in the United States. These include denying boarding to unauthorized visitors, requiring photographic identification cards for officers and crew members, conducting metal-detector screening of all boarding passengers, randomly inspecting hand-carried baggage and ship's stores (food and supplies loaded in port), and restricting access to the ship's bridge, engine room, and radio room.

With a medium risk of a terrorist attack, cruise lines are required to search at least half of all ship's stores, embarking passengers, and carry-on baggage, as well as to provide passengers with photo identification cards. At the highest risk level, all passengers and all baggage, both carry-on and checked-in, must be inspected. In addition, the targeted cruise ship has the option of bypassing any scheduled port of call where terrorists are expected to strike.

The ICCL Assures Congress But Misstates the Facts

On October 2, 2001, International Council of Cruise Lines (ICCL) president Michael Crye testified on security issues before the Senate Subcommittee on Surface Transportation and Merchant Marine of the Commerce, Science and Transportation Committee. He assured the committee that since the September 11th attack on the World Trade Center and the Pentagon, the cruise industry was operating at level-three security.[20] Committee members were appropriately impressed.

However, I had visited a ship in port at St. John's, Newfoundland, several days before Crye testified and observed that even the less stringent security requirements under level two weren't being observed. Passengers were not required to have photo identification, and few if any carry-on items were being inspected. I walked aboard with a briefcase that was neither scanned nor opened.

To regain entry to the ship, passengers were asked to show only their room key — no photo identification — and for a substantial amount of time (because of a computer malfunction), the safety officer simply wrote down the names of people as they left and checked them off when they returned. While Michael Crye boasted about the passenger-access control system used by most cruise ships to monitor access to the ship, the 2,000-passenger ship I boarded had none.

The system, also called A-PASS (Automated Personnel Assisted Security Screening), provides high-speed, interactive photo identification and screening of passengers and crew as they enter and exit a ship. Prior to embarking, passengers stop at a kiosk, insert their shipboard identification card, and have their picture taken by a camera within the kiosk. Thereafter, each time passengers exit or enter the ship, they insert their card into a kiosk located near the ship's gangway, where the time of entry or exit is recorded. As well, the safety officer stationed at the gangway matches the photograph on the computer with the person. The system allows ship personnel to know, at any point in time, who is aboard the ship and who is off. Together with automated locks on cabins that record each entry to and exit from a cabin, and the increasing use of surveillance cameras throughout the ship, personnel are able to keep track of the comings and goings of most passengers.

Photo ID System at Mercy of Human Error

These sophisticated security systems are, however, at the mercy of human error. Here's an example. In July 2000 a nine-year-old autistic boy wandered onto Carnival Cruise Line's *Sensation* while it was visiting New Orleans as part of a seven-day cruise from Tampa. He somehow got past customs officials and ship employees, boarding the ship with a woman who had a group of children. The woman showed her ship-issued identification card, said the children were with her, and the group was allowed to pass. It wasn't until midnight that crew realized the youngster was not actually part of any group and began the process of trying to identify him. This was difficult because the boy was uncommunicative and had no identification, and the missing person report filed with the New Orleans police had been misplaced. Two days later when the ship reached Tampa, the boy was taken into custody by authorities, and another day later he was finally reunited with his mother.

In another incident two months later, a woman was reported missing from Princess Cruises' *Dawn Princess* on its Alaska itinerary. The room steward reported her absence when he entered to clean her room and found that she hadn't slept in the bed. Because the A-PASS system did not indicate that she had disembarked, crew assumed she must have fallen overboard sometime between 4:30 the afternoon before (when she was last seen) and 8:30 that morning (when she was noticed missing). The Coast Guard was notified and a search was undertaken. A day later the woman was located — at her home in Michigan. She had left the ship in Juneau because of a disagreement with her traveling companion.

Despite public assurances and security policies, a ship is still vulnerable. On a cruise in December 2001 — less than three months after the events of September 11 — I noticed that the security zone required for heightened security measures was not always maintained around the ship. Most passengers never even think about the inherent security risks associated with a cruise.

The Risk of Assault

Although relatively uncommon in terms of the number of passenger days, the risk of assault exists on cruise ships. "Gay bashing" has been reported on a number of cruises where a group of gays was mixed with straight single men. As well, there are occasional reports of altercations between passengers, often with one or both in a state of intoxication. A cruise ship is a microcosm of the larger society. The problems that are common on land follow you onto the seas.

Do You Know Where Your Children Are?

Almost every year there are one or two media reports of children being sexually assaulted onboard a cruise ship. How common these occurrences are is hard to tell.

One problem is that cruise lines tend to avoid reporting physical and sexual assaults. Although the FBI and Coast Guard are authorized to investigate and prosecute any alleged crimes involving American citizens in international waters, and IMO security guidelines require that the operator of a vessel report each unlawful act, until 1999 there was ambiguity about the definition of "unlawful." According to a related story in the *New York Times*:

> Cruise ships are required to report only crimes and other incidents that result in serious physical injury, which does not necessarily include rape. "Unless otherwise required to do so, Carnival [Cruise Line] leaves it to the individual to decide to report to authorities," said Curtis Mase, a lawyer for Carnival.[21]

A second problem is that reporting may be discouraged by fear of secondary victimization. Parents may avoid reporting cases involving their children. This fear is quite real. Royal Caribbean Cruise Line's defense in a lawsuit following the rape of a 16-year-old girl in 1995 suggested the girl's parents were to blame for the rape because they had failed to exercise reasonable care in protecting their daughter. Interestingly, in December 2000 the cruise line introduced its "New Adventure Ocean Dining Program" under which children sailing on any Royal Caribbean ship — there are on average 120,000 child passengers per year — can now dine with their favorite youth staff. Whether the company would now accept responsibility if something happened is unclear.

The first molestation case to receive considerable attention — it was the first time that a cruise line crew member had gone to trial — involved the rape in August 1989 of a 14-year-old girl on Carnival Cruise Line's *Carnivale*. According to testimony at the trial, as the ship was returning to Miami from the Bahamas the 14-year-old girl went to the family's cabin, while other family members remained on deck, at 5:30 a.m. to check on a suitcase. While she was in the elevator, a male crew member (a cleaner aboard the ship) kissed and fondled her. He then dragged her from the elevator to a cleaning closet and raped her on the floor. The girl picked the 32-year-old crewman, a Colombian national and father of two, out of a lineup. In February 1990 he was found guilty of the charges and sentenced to 30 years in prison.[22]

Since then additional cases involving children have been reported. In 1991 a 12-year-old girl was fondled in the elevator of Carnival Cruise Line's *Jubilee*. The perpetrator was never found. In 1992 a 15-year-old girl was raped on Windjammer Cruises' *Fantome*. At the time none of the cabins had doors that locked, so the crewman easily gained entry. A 1995 news article reported an incident in which a crewman broke into a cabin and raped two girls under the age of 10. A year earlier, in 1994, a crewman on Dolphin Cruises' *Seabreeze* molested a 13-year-old boy. In both of the latter cases, the offenders were identified but it is unclear whether they were prosecuted for the crime.

Between 1995 and 2000 the media reported at least eight cases involving children. A 16-year-old girl celebrating her birthday was raped on Royal Caribbean Cruise Line's *Monarch of the Seas* after striking up a conversation with a bartender who later was her attacker.[23] A 14-year-old girl and a 16-year-old girl were both raped, in separate incidents several weeks apart in 1996, by the same crewman aboard Carnival Cruise Line's *Fascination* — the latter case only came to light because of publicity from the first.[24] A 13-year-old child was the victim of an attempted sexual assault by a 30-year-old passenger in 1997 aboard Premier Cruises' *Atlantica*. A 15-year-old boy was molested in 1998 by a bartender on a Royal Caribbean Cruise Line ship after he was served more than a dozen glasses of champagne and then taken to an empty cabin where he was stripped and sexually assaulted.[25] And in 1999, a 13-year-old girl was assaulted by a waiter aboard Celebrity's Cruises' *Galaxy*, and a 12-year-old boy was molested by a kitchen steward aboard a ship belonging to Norwegian Cruise Lines.

In October 2000 a 30-year-old youth coordinator on Norwegian Cruise Line's *Norway* was arrested and charged with sexually assaulting a 12-year-old girl who had come with him to his cabin. In this last case, the parents are suing Norwegian Cruise Line for not properly screening their employees: the youth coordinator had an arrest record that included indecent exposure.[26]

Because most passengers have no idea that this type of thing happens onboard cruise ships, many parents let their children run free. They naively believe there is nothing to fear — but a ship must be treated like any urban setting. As an FBI agent in Miami said, "Even out at sea, you can't let your guard down."

Sexual Assaults on Women

Sexual assaults are not limited to children. Again, it's difficult to get a clear picture of the problem because it is so well concealed. Even though Carnival Cruise Line and Royal Caribbean International together admitted to receiving reports of 166 sexual assaults in the five-year period from August 1994 through August 1998, only a few cases have been reported in the media. Next to none of them involved passenger-on-passenger assaults.[27]

An early glimpse of the problem is reflected in a letter to the editor of the *Los Angeles Times* in 1991.[29] The writer, a 40-year-old woman who had recently returned from a cruise with her mother, warns single women about what awaits them on such a vacation. She describes being propositioned by her cabin steward and relentlessly pursued by a dining room waiter who wouldn't take no for an answer. Enjoyment of her cruise was compromised, and she was forced to remain in the company of others for self-protection. In her case, the experience was harassment. But sometimes it goes further.

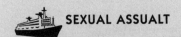 **SEXUAL ASSUALT**

Between August 1994 and August 1998, Carnival Cruise Line received 108 complaints of sexual assault. Royal Caribbean Cruise Line reported 58 sexual assaults over the same period.[28]

In 1990 a passenger with Carnival Cruise Line accused her cabin steward of entering her cabin while she was asleep. He climbed on top of her and fondled her, but was scared away when the woman and her roommate both began screaming. The woman reported the incident to the ship's safety officer, but nothing happened.

In 1992 a 31-year-old woman traveling on Carnival Cruise Line's *Festivale* claimed that a waiter had sneaked into her cabin while she was getting dressed in the bathroom. She filed a report with the Barbados police, but again nothing happened. Neither the woman nor Carnival contacted the FBI. The woman launched a lawsuit against Carnival Cruise Lines, which was settled out of court.[30]

In 1993 a 62-year-old woman on Seawind Cruise Line's *Seawind Crown* was strangled to death following a failed rape attempt when she was using a public toilet at 9:00 a.m. The two crewmen were caught because they were seen throwing the body overboard as the ship left the Aruba harbor. They were detained and went to trial in Aruba.[31]

In June 1997 a 35-year-old woman aboard Royal Caribbean Cruise Line's *Majesty of the Seas* claimed she was raped after returning from the nightclub at 4:00 a.m., where she had consumed only nonalcoholic beverages. She said she had been attacked by a member of the cleaning crew, and she picked the man out of a lineup conducted by the ship's security officers. Questioned by the ship's security officer and a company lawyer who had flown in, the worker denied being anywhere near a passenger. He said he had been washing decks — at 4:00 in the morning — and attributed the scratches on his body to minor work accidents. He was indicted, and as his trial approached, DNA evidence linked him to the assault. The crewman then switched his story; his lawyers argued that the woman had consented to sex. Because she had filed for bankruptcy just before going on the cruise, they suggested the lawsuit against Royal Caribbean Cruise Line had been planned. After four hours of deliberation, a jury acquitted the alleged attacker.[32] In court papers, Royal Caribbean said it "was not responsible for a crew member's actions outside his official duties."[33]

In 1998 two cases against Carnival Cruise Lines were reported. In one, a woman on a Caribbean cruise with her husband accused a waiter of drugging their dinner drinks and later raping her in their cabin as her husband lay unconscious. The couple complained to cruise officials, who responded in part by moving them to a better cabin for the remainder of the cruise. The case was settled just before it was set to go to trial.[35] In the other case, a woman traveling with her mother claimed a room steward had raped her. "She asserts ... [he]

> "According to US Justice Department figures, one in three crimes reported at sea is the crime of rape. That's rarely noted in travel brochures."[34]
>
> — Nickie McWhirter, Detroit News, August 29, 1995

pushed her down on one of the beds and raped her. She reported the incident immediately to ship personnel, who questioned [the steward]. He denied the charge."[36] The disposition of that case is unknown.

In 2000 two young women on separate cruises with Premier Cruises reported being raped by the same 30-year-old employee. In one case, the passenger was returning to the disco from her cabin. She asked a crew member for directions; he proceeded to lead her down a dead end and then sexually assaulted her. Although immediately fired and confined to his cabin, the crew member was not turned over to American authorities when the ship returned to Boston.

Also in 2000 a 40-year-old woman was raped in a restroom aboard the *SeaEscape* by another passenger. Her attacker was not found.

Socializing: Rules versus Practice

Policies prohibiting crew from socializing with passengers are often ignored; there are many cases of consensual relationships involving passengers and crew. Only when there is an attack or a complaint are policies prohibiting these contacts apparently enforced. The usual situation, according to a musician who worked for both Carnival Cruise Line and Royal Caribbean Cruise Line, is that "sex between crew and passengers happens all the time. Every cruise, every day. Crew go into guest cabins and guests go to crew cabins. Both seek it out, passengers and crew." A bartender employed by Carnival Cruise Line suggests that crew members make a sport of having sex with passengers, describing the practice as simply "part of the game."[39]

 BAD BILL

In 1995 the House of Representatives passed House Resolution 1361 with no hearings and no debate. According to the Association of Trial Lawyers of America, the bill would have permitted substandard medical care for passengers and crew and would have jeopardized the legal rights of passengers who became victims of crimes, including rape, onboard cruise ships. The bill would allow any cruise ship and its parent line to limit any liability for emotional and psychological injuries to passengers by simply printing a disclaimer in the cruise contract.[37] South Carolina senator Ernest Hollings stopped the legislation after lobbyists for the trial lawyers started a campaign against it. The bill had been introduced by Alaska congressman Don Young, who between 1993 and 1998 received at least $29,000 from political action committees and individuals affiliated with the cruise industry.[38]

Although cruise lines have policies that prohibit crew from fraternizing with passengers, there are not similar policies for officers and staff. In fact, officers are in many cases urged to socialize with passengers. However "socializing" is subject to different interpretations, and in many cases it isn't limited to a drink and a dance.

According to a woman who worked on a cruise ship for five years:

Some officers were notorious womanizers. In my first weeks at sea, I was so naive that I actually visited an officer's cabin and admired his photos of his beautiful blond sister — before realizing that she was really his wife.

I got wise. Others didn't. One passenger had been swept off her feet, on an earlier cruise, by a chief engineer ... and though he was no longer with the company, she always insisted on being seated, for nostalgic reasons, at the chief [engineer]'s table in the dining room.

Officers usually relished female attention, but a few had to dodge unwanted advances. One engineer locked himself in his cabin for an entire cruise to avoid a young woman he had wooed on a previous sailing; she had returned with her mother, who was talking marriage. As an escape trick, some officers would arrange in advance to be paged at a certain time. "My beeper," they'll tell a lovesick lady as they dashed off the dance floor. "Duty calls."[40]

Under the Microscope: The New Zero-Tolerance Policy

Disclosures of sexual assaults brought considerable media attention to the way in which cruise lines dealt with assaults. This led four companies — Carnival Corporation, Royal Caribbean Cruises Limited, Crystal Cruises, and Princess Cruises — to sign a letter in July 1999, under the auspices of the ICCL, pledging zero tolerance of crime and a commitment to report all crimes involving American citizens to the FBI. Whether crimes against non-American citizens will be reported remains unclear two and a half years later.

A 1998 *New York Times* article describes the pattern of response common at that time. Based on examination of court records and on interviews with cruise line employees, law enforcement officials, and passengers and their lawyers, the article suggested that there was

a pattern of cover-ups that often began as soon as the crime was reported at sea, in international waters where the only police are the ship's security officers. Accused crewmembers are sometimes put ashore at the next port, with airfare to their home country. Industry lawyers are flown to the ship to question the accusers; and aboard ships flowing with liquor, counterclaims of consensual sex are common. The cruise lines aggressively contest lawsuits and insist on secrecy as a condition of settling.[41]

According to a former chief of security for Carnival Cruise Line:

> You don't notify the FBI. You don't notify anybody. You start giving the victims bribes, upgrading their cabins, giving them champagne and trying to ease them off the ship until the legal department can take over. Even when I knew there was a crime, I was supposed to go in there and do everything in the world to get Carnival to look innocent.[42]

Once a crime is reported, there are problems with preserving evidence. Cabins are routinely cleaned twice a day, so much evidence is destroyed very quickly, and there is often a significant delay between the time of an attack and landing at a American port. Rape experts suggest that cases reported within 72 hours provide the best forensic evidence, but this time frame is difficult for attacks that occur on a cruise ship. In addition, many victims are likely to delay making a report as long as they are aboard a ship because of fear of reprisal and because there is no independent investigator or rape-treatment centre. Simply put, rapes on cruise ships are often not reported until it is too late for criminal investigation.

Even in cases where a sexual assault is reported in a timely manner, victims and prosecutors are faced with the common practice of cruise lines immediately sending the accused crew member back home, purportedly because he has violated company policies that prohibit fraternizing between passengers and crew. Reporters for the *Miami New Times* found that in each of five lawsuits against Carnival Cruise Line they reviewed, the employee was swept out of the country immediately after the ship arrived in port. In one case, the employee was later rehired by the company; he was subsequently served with a summons while at the dock in Los Angeles. Carnival's lawyers successfully argued the Indian citizen couldn't be sued in American courts because American laws did not apply to him: not only was he a foreigner, but the alleged crime took place in Barbados on a ship registered in Panama. The passenger's lawsuit against Carnival Cruise Line was settled out of court.[43]

It remains to be seen whether these patterns continue under the cruise industry's "zero tolerance" pledge. Sadly, "zero tolerance" seems to refer to how cases of rape are handled once reported; it does not reduce the risk of assault nor make reporting an attack any easier.

AVOIDING UNNECESSARY ILLNESS

I have been fortunate on the cruises I have taken. Other than the results of overeating, I have avoided gastrointestinal illness. Many times I have seen colds and influenzas spread like wildfire among passengers, and I've met a significant number of passengers who have suffered gastrointestinal ailments resulting from contaminated or improperly stored food.

Many cruise passengers rely on the US Centers for Disease Control (CDC) to ensure safe and sanitary conditions. After several major disease outbreaks on cruise ships, the CDC initiated its Vessel Sanitation Program in cooperation with the cruise industry. The program's primary goal is to lower the risk of gastrointestinal and other disease outbreaks on cruise ships.

Twice a year, Vessel Sanitation Program staff conduct surprise inspections of cruise ships visiting American ports. The inspection focuses on such things as the ship's food and water supply, the "practices and personal hygiene of employees," the "general cleanliness and physical condition of the ship," and "the ship's training programs." A ship is scored for its compliance on 41 items; the passing mark is 86 points out of 100. When a ship fails to pass inspection, a follow-up inspection is conducted within 30 to 60 days.

The CDC's Vessel Sanitation Program has had positive results. In the 1970s and 1980s, cruise ships suffered 12 to 15 outbreaks of gastroenteritis (or similar illness) every year. By the early 1990s the number had decreased and was down to 10 outbreaks in 1997 and 9 in 1998.

While the number of outbreaks of gastrointestinal illness aboard cruise ships has decreased, the proportion of outbreaks caused by contaminated food or water (rather than by person-to-person contact) has increased. The proportion of food and water contamination caused by agents such as salmonella and shigellosis have remained constant over time, but the percentage of outbreaks caused by Norwalk-like viruses have increased to one-third of all cases.[44]

Passengers commonly use CDC sanitation inspection scores as a definitive guide to the "health" of a cruise ship. The scores do provide some insight — but no guarantee. The simple fact is that ships with passing scores still have violations; many violations do not result in point deductions. For example, I checked the Vessel Sanitation Program report posted on the Internet prior to going on a cruise aboard the *Radisson Diamond*; the ship had received a passing score of 93. The complete report, however, indicated serious problems with the water purification system, that an adult

 DOES A PERFECT SCORE MEAN PERFECTION?

An inspection of Radisson's Seven Seas Navigator conducted March 29, 2001, under the Vessel Sanitation Program is instructive. The ship received a perfect score of 100 — but the report indicated a range of violations, including:

- the bacteriological kits [used to test potable water] were not of an approved type
- the potable water lines to the spray hose and pulper [in the Lido pot wash] were not fitted with backflow prevention devices
- backflow prevention devices were not provided on the ware washing units [at the pool grill]
- the precautions and risks sign [at the spa] did not caution immunocompromised individuals
- a large wheel of cheese that had been sliced was not dated
- cold cuts [at the Lido buffet] were tested at 47° F. [The recommendation is that] potentially hazardous food shall be maintained: (1) at 60° C (140° F) ... or above; or (2) at 5° C (41° F) or less

cockroach had been seen in an oven, and that a pest-control device located in the galley posed a risk of food contamination. This information was more descriptive and helpful than was the overall score.

Canada conducts sanitary inspections similar to those done in the United States. In the United Kingdom, the Food Standards Agency announced in May 2001 its plan to give health officials the statutory right to enter and inspect cruise ships. This followed an increase of food poisoning cases among cruise passengers and a report by the UK Consumers' Association that in the previous two years it had received complaints about 14 cruise ships, with passengers contracting illnesses ranging from salmonella poisoning to the potentially fatal Legionnaire's disease.[46]

- the ware washing units [at the Pool Grill] were not provided with data plates
- the main dishwasher [in the galley] did not have a data plate
- the main dishwasher temperature gauges were 30 to 60° out of calibration
- none of the pot wash staff knew the new halogen sanitizing time requirements
- some clean bread baskets [in the Lido dining room] were soiled with bread crumbs
- the clean storage racks [at the Pool Grill] were soiled
- some mold was noted in the technical space underneath the sink [at the Pool Grill]
- training was not documented in the IPM [integrated pest management] plan
- the cleaning schedule for the air handling ventilation units did not include the condensate collection system.

Source: Centers for Disease Control, Vessel Sanitation Program website[45]

Note: To remain as accurate as possible to the actual report, the language used in the Vessel Sanitation Program inspection report has been retained. Each point listed above summarizes a separate violation, including its nature and site. The full report includes recommendations to the cruise line.

Is the Food Safe to Eat?

In December 2001 a cruise ship worker told me about an investigation done in the UK following a gastrointestinal outbreak on a cruise ship. Inspectors had taken samples from food products onboard and determined a common contact source for all food that showed contamination. The cause? A baker in the galley had not been washing his hands after using the washroom.

Sanitary inspection scores are not a reliable indicator of risk. Certainly, there are cases where a ship fails its sanitation inspection immediately following an outbreak of disease. But there have also been disease outbreaks within weeks of ships passing their inspection,[47] as well as cases of ships with no reported illness despite a failing score. In July 2001 the *Arcadia* was issued a no-sail order following several warnings and finally being given a failing score of 59 on its sanitation inspection. The CDC cited poor food refrigeration, a dirty kitchen, and failure to guarantee potable water.

 SOURCES OF FOODBORNE ILLNESS

Inadequate time and temperature during food storage and preparation — refrigeration and cooking — are contributing factors to foodborne illness. A related article in the *Cruise Industry News Quarterly* presented historical data collected from the United States, Canada, and England, with a breakdown of the relative frequency of key factors:[48]

- 63% — inadequate cooling and cold holding [refrigeration]
- 29% — preparing food ahead of schedule
- 27% — inadequate pot holding
- 26% — poor personal hygiene; infected person
- 25% — inadequate reheating
- 9% — inadequate cleaning of equipment
- 5% — inadequate cooking or heat process
- 4% — [storage] containers adding toxic chemicals
- 2% — contaminated raw ingredients
- 2% — intentional chemical additives
- 1% — incidental chemical additives
- 1% — unsafe sources

Take some solace in the fact that disease outbreaks are relatively infrequent — in 1997 there were a mere 2.1 outbreaks for every ten million passenger days. That's four times lower than between 1975 and 1979, when the rate of outbreak was 8.1 per ten million passenger days. Regardless, the risk is still present and real.

What Unseen Risk Is in Your Food?

The two most common causes of foodborne illness are food contamination and the Norwalk-like virus. In comparison the incidence of enterotoxigenic *Escherichia coli (E. coli)* and *Shigella* is relatively low.

However, an April 2000 article warns that *E. coli* is an increasing risk to those on cruise ships. After a study of outbreaks of gastrointestinal disease on three cruises in 1997-98, researchers determined that in each case the source of *E. coli* appeared to be contaminated water taken on the ship in foreign ports. The 1,300 affected passengers had been infected by drinking beverages with ice cubes or by consuming unbottled water. Although cruise ships have water treatment plants designed to avoid these problems, it was believed that the shipboard water treatment system "had briefly failed."[49]

In the year 2000 the CDC studied four outbreaks of gastroenteritis on ships based in American ports, two of which were traced to bacterial contamination of shrimp and other seafood. All indications were that the contamination of the shrimp had occurred in the factory rather than on the cruise ship.[50]

The other two outbreaks were attributed to the Norwalk-like virus, but in neither case was the source identified. In one case, the investigation noted deficiencies that, although not directly responsible for transmission of the virus, could have allowed its survival.[51] In the other case, the relatively low number of unaffected passengers and crew made it difficult to identify a single point of contamination. Investigators suggested both drinking water and cut fruits and vegetables washed in the drinking water as possible sources.[52]

Other than the no-sail order issued for the *Arcadia* in 2001, only one media report that year involved foodborne illness on a cruise ship. In August 2001 the Liberian-registered *Switzerland* (owned by a subsidiary of Swissair and leased to Leisure Cruises), on a cruise beginning in the Netherlands, had a salmonella outbreak that affected more than 100 of the 600 passengers and sent 20 people to hospital.

 NORWALK-LIKE VIRUS DEFINED

Among the most common causes of foodborne illness, the Norwalk virus and/or Norwalk-like virus (named after Norwalk, Ohio, where the first outbreak was documented in a school cafeteria) belong to a family of unclassified, small, round-structured viruses that cause a mild and brief illness with nausea, vomiting, diarrhea, abdominal pain, and sometimes also a headache and low-grade fever. Symptoms begin one to two days after eating contaminated food or water and last for another couple of days. The Norwalk virus can be transmitted through water, shellfish (eating raw or insufficiently steamed clams and oysters poses a high risk of infection by the Norwalk virus), salad ingredients, and anything prepared by an infected food handler.

Several ships in recent years have had serious Norwalk virus outbreaks. In 1997 there were outbreaks on three successive cruises of Norwegian Cruise Line's *Royal Odyssey*. Following a "Recommendation Not to Sail" by the Centers for Disease Control (CDC), the *Royal Odyssey* was pulled from service a week earlier than planned, sanitized, and refit as the *Norwegian Star*. In 1998 Princess Cruises' *Regal Princess* had three successive cruises with gastrointestinal illness traced to the Norwalk virus. The ship was pulled from service for a week and completely sanitized. In 2000 Clipper Cruise Line's *Nantucket Clipper* was taken from service following an outbreak on two cruises. It was cleaned, returned to service, and had another outbreak on the first cruise, requiring it to again be pulled from service, and again sanitized.[53]

Onshore Catering and Foodborne Illness

An Australian study published in January 2001 reported on risks associated with food eaten by cruise ship passengers while ashore. It found that passengers who ate onshore had a significantly higher risk of developing diarrhea than those who did not. In addition, passengers who ate while on a tour were at greater risk than those who did not go on a tour. The study supported a 1996 report in the *Journal of the American Medical Association* which estimated that one-third of gastrointestinal outbreaks on cruise ships might be prevented if onshore caterers were not used for off-ship excursions. The Australian study suggests that meals served as part of a ship-sponsored shore excursion are a greater risk than those purchased on your own.[54]

An Unhealthy Environment?

The most common non-foodborne illnesses on a cruise ship are colds and flu. The cruise ship is an ideal incubator for these common afflictions. It provides a confined area, and people are engaged in almost nonstop socializing. During the 1998 season more than 2,100 cases of flu were reported among passengers and crew on Alaska cruises.[55]

There have been some large-scale flu outbreaks. In several cases the initial fear was for Legionnaire's disease, but that was ultimately ruled out in a 1997 influenza outbreak striking passengers on successive sailings of Holland America Line's Westerdam.[56] It was also eliminated the following year as the cause of a large gastrointestinal disease outbreak on the *Regal Princess* — the cause was found to be the Norwalk-like virus.[57] *Legionella* (the bacterium that causes Legionnaire's disease) was also eliminated as the cause of two passengers dying from illness contracted on P&O's *Fair Princess* in September 2000, but the exact cause of the deaths and of dozens falling ill remains a mystery.

Legionnaire's Disease

According to a 1998 article, more than 100 cases of Legionnaire's disease, resulting in ten deaths, have been linked to ships — mostly cruise ships.[58] The most widely known outbreak was on Celebrity Cruises' *Horizon* in 1994. On ten different cruises on that ship, 16 passengers were confirmed to have Legionnaire's disease and another 34 cases were suspected. One person died and four people required intensive treatment on ventilators. The source was traced to the outdoor whirlpool spa.[59] One year later the same ship had an outbreak of salmonella that struck 220 passengers.[60]

In 1998 two cases of Legionnaire's disease occurred on Direct Cruises' *Edinburgh Castle*, which was operating in the UK. The problem was traced to the water purification system — the first time a water supply system was implicated in transmission of this disease.[61] The system was disinfected and the ship was placed back into service.

But overall, ship-associated cases of Legionnaire's disease are rare. Most studies recommend that ship owners, operators, and captains be diligent in maintaining the water and air-conditioning systems on their vessels. Whirlpool spas are identified as requiring particular care and maintenance.

Pregnant Women Beware

In 1998 the Canadian Medical Association issued a warning on the risks of rubella (German measles) infection aboard cruise ships, after a similar advisory from the US Centers for Disease Control (CDC).[62] Before going on a cruise, women of childbearing ages were advised to have their immunity to the disease checked, and if necessary, to be vaccinated.[63]

This advisory followed several outbreaks of rubella on cruise ships. The CDC estimated that 75 percent of the crew members on a ship were susceptible to rubella — consequently a case of the disease within the confined environment of a cruise ship would pose a serious threat to passengers. Based on the number of female cruise ship passengers who were pregnant and/or of childbearing age, the CDC stated that one case of congenital rubella syndrome could occur every week during an onboard outbreak. Congenital rubella syndrome can result in severe birth defects, including deafness, cataracts, heart defects, and mental retardation.

However, the cruise industry says vaccinating its employees against rubella — thus protecting passengers — would be too expensive. The medical director for Holland America Line suggested it would cost $600,000 to inoculate all crew on Holland America Line and Windstar Cruises.[64]

More Health Risks

Dirt and lint in ventilation ducts present health risks, including aggravation of allergies and a breeding ground for airborne organisms. These ducts gather an incredible amount of lint, dirt, dust, and debris — one aircraft carrier has an estimated 60 tons of debris in its vent ducts, according to a study by the US Navy. The dirtiest ducts are in the laundry, the galley, and accommodation areas, in that order.[65] And this debris poses a health risk and a risk to safety. A series of recommendations regarding lint in laundry vents followed the National Transportation Safety Board investigation of the 1998 fire aboard Carnival Cruise Line's *Ecstasy*.[66]

As in any social setting, risks of disease exist onboard cruise ships. The public only becomes aware of the problem after something happens. For example, in January 2002 Australian health officials issued an urgent warning to hundreds of passengers returning from a nine-night cruise on P&O's *Pacific Sky*. Within a week of the cruise's end, a young man in Sydney had died from meningitis and another passenger in Adelaide was hospitalized and diagnosed with the same illness.[67]

Granted, communicable diseases are spread every day in varieties of settings. However, cruise ships present a unique situation because of the closed nature of the environment and the high level of social interaction among passengers.

MEDICAL CARE IS NOT REQUIRED

Surprisingly, international maritime law does not explicitly require that a cruise ship provide medical services. However, International Labor Organization Convention 164, entitled "Health Protection and Medical Care for Seafarers," requires that ships "engaged in international voyages of more than three days' duration shall carry a medical doctor as a member of the crew responsible for providing medical care." Another related legal requirement is set forth in the International Convention on Standards of Training, Certification and Watchkeeping for Seafarers (SCTW), which stipulates only that certain crew members have various levels of first-aid and medical training.

Regardless, all modern cruise ships do maintain an infirmary. The people dispensing onboard medical care are concessionaires, and the cruise line assumes no liability for their actions. Their precise qualifications can vary widely, too. Some small cruise ships may have a nurse but no doctor; some large ships may have two doctors as well as two or more nurses.

In 1996 the ICCL adopted industry guidelines for medical facilities and personnel on cruise ships. The guidelines were a response to pressure from the American Medical Association (AMA), which had that year called on Congress urging the development of medical standards for cruise ships. Based on a number of cases of disease, including an outbreak of gastroenteritis that year on Carnival Cruise Line's *Jubilee* in which 150 passengers became ill and one person died, the AMA also called for greater awareness of the limited medical services available aboard ships. The AMA position was supported by a survey administered by two Florida doctors to 11 cruise lines.

> The doctors found that 27 percent of doctors and nurses did not have advanced training in treating victims of heart attacks, the leading killer on ships, and 54 percent of doctors and 72 percent of nurses lacked advanced training for dealing with trauma. Fewer than half of shipboard doctors — 45 percent — had board certification, an important credential that is granted after three to seven years of residency and a written examination in a specialty or its equivalent.... As for equipment, the survey found that 63 percent of ships did not have equipment for blood tests for diagnosing heart attacks, and 45 percent did not have mechanical ventilators or external pacemakers. "What we found was that the quality of maritime medical care was less than adequate, from the medical facilities to nurse and physician credentials."[68]

The AMA has continued to lobby for government regulation of health care on cruise ships, but to date without success.

Are ICCL Guidelines for Medical Care Enough?

In May 2000, when I was sailing on the *Radisson Diamond*, I was given a tour of the ship's infirmary. Spotting a sign on a door that read "Caution: X ray in Use," I commented that I was impressed to see that the ship had an X-ray machine — equipment not technically required for a ship of the *Diamond*'s size and age. My impression shifted from positive to negative, however, when I was told that the X-ray machine had broken down a number of years ago and had never been repaired, presumably because of the cost. The X-ray room was now an all-purpose storage closet.

Most cruise lines marketed to North Americans subscribe to ICCL guidelines for medical facilities and medical staff. These guidelines are entirely voluntary and are not intended to establish standards of care for the industry: "They simply reflect a consensus among member lines of the facilities and staffing needs considered appropriate aboard cruise vessels."[69]

The ICCL guidelines suggest that ships have onboard one infirmary bed per 1,000 passengers and crew, and one intensive-care-unit bed per ship. As well, the guidelines recommend having a variety of equipment, including two cardiac monitors; two defibrillators; an electrocardiograph (ECG); advanced life support medications sufficient to run two complex codes; capability for measurement of hemoglobin/hemocrit, urinalysis, pregnancy tests, and glucose tests; X-ray machines onboard ships delivered after January 1, 1997, with capacity for more than 1,000 passengers; and a range of emergency medications and supplies. Despite these recommendations, the actual equipment onboard varies depending upon the itinerary, size of the ship, and anticipated demographic makeup of passengers.

Infirmaries on ships are equipped to deal with minor injuries, including workplace injuries of crew. They are also able to stabilize a patient having a heart attack or suffering other acute conditions. But realistically, the ship's infirmary is more like a neighborhood clinic than a hospital emergency room. It can deal most effectively with routine problems such as scrapes and cuts, sunburn, and indigestion. It also is equipped to serve as the "family doctor" for all the ship's crew, treating anything from a common cold or flu to high blood sugar or hypertension.

By necessity, the infirmary also deals with emergency situations. Ninety percent of the 60 onboard deaths reported by cruise ships sailing out of Miami between September 1996 and September 1999 were attributed to a heart attack or heart-related problems. With a fleet of seven ships at the time, Holland America Line indicated in 1996 that it had between 325 and 375 emergency evacuations — 40 by air ambulance — per year.[70] These numbers, applied industry-wide, suggest that there could have been as many as 4,000 evacuations in 1996 and potentially more than 6,000 in 2001.

Meet the Medical Staff

The training and background of medical personnel varies widely. Several cruise lines, such as Holland America Line, Princess Cruises, and Norwegian Cruise Line, draw their physicians only from the United Kingdom, the United States, and/or Canada, and pay salaries of $8,000 to $10,000 a month; all physicians are board-certified in one of these countries. In contrast, some cruise lines hire medical personnel from a range of countries and pay salaries reportedly as low as $1,057 a month; often those hired are not board-certified. A 1999 *New York Times* article reports that only 56 percent of the doctors on Carnival Cruise Line's ships had board certification or equivalent, while 85 percent of the physicians on Royal Caribbean Cruise Lines were board-certified.[71]

Board certification in itself may not be altogether reassuring. I knew a physician on one cruise ship whose 30 years of practice had been as an anesthesiologist; his ability to deal with some of the potential emergency situations on a cruise ship was untested. I met another physician whose specialty was oncological colorectal surgery. Although well respected within his specialization, he had not been regularly required to exercise the skills needed in emergency medicine.

ICCL guidelines recommend that medical staff are skilled in advanced life support and cardiac care; they do not, however, require that medical personnel be certified in Advanced Cardiac Life Support (ACLS) — a standard requirement for any doctor working in emergency medicine in North America. There is a wide difference between claiming a skill and demonstrating that skill through recertification, which for ACLS is required every three years.

Recent technology has brought telemedicine systems — satellite hook-ups from the ship to a medical center ashore — onboard cruise ships. These systems provide expertise that may not otherwise be available aboard the ship. For example, Princess Cruises' MedServe program provides a link with onshore radiology experts who provide diagnostic support on all X-ray images taken onboard; the program is being expanded to include other medical specialties. The system runs on a cost recovery basis with a consultation beginning at $500. In the system's first year of operation, 300 telemedicine consultations were conducted.

Code Alpha and Other Medical Emergencies

Medical staff onboard a ship deal with both routine and emergency situations, and in most cases, the required treatment is provided. But there have been times when medical care has fallen short. A two-part 1999 *New York Times* article discusses several of these cases.[72]

In one, the doctor on the Carnival *Ecstasy* failed to diagnose a 14-year-old girl whose appendix had ruptured, causing a massive infection. After the third visit and the doctor's continued assurances that the problem was not the girl's appendix, the parents contacted their family physician. On his advice, they returned home midway through the cruise. The daughter underwent emergency surgery and will have lifelong medical problems as a result of the infection from a ruptured appendix.

In another case, a woman and her husband were on Carnival Cruise Line's *Sensation* for their honeymoon. They returned to the ship from a walk ashore and headed to the infirmary because the woman, a diabetic, felt flushed. The nurse and doctor checked her blood sugar and because it was very high, administered fast-acting insulin to bring the blood sugar down. The husband recalled, "Instead of getting better, she got worse and worse.... She was totally unconscious and went into a diabetic coma and was wringing wet. I called for the nurse and she said she'd come around. I waited and she started jerking real bad."[73]

He rushed back to their cabin to get his wife's glucose meter and returned to the infirmary to measure her blood sugar himself. He found that her blood sugar was not too high but rather, too low. The nurse administered glucose and the woman regained consciousness about 15 minutes later. The couple claims that the incident caused brain damage, leaving the woman disoriented and unable to return to her job.

Still another case involved a 47-year-old woman on Celebrity Cruises' *Zenith*, who went to the infirmary complaining of difficulty breathing and chest pain. The physician took a chest X ray and diagnosed an upper-respiratory tract infection and acute bronchitis. Because her condition failed to improve over the next three days, she made additional visits to the doctor. After the cruise ended, she returned to New York and was hospitalized the following day. She died in intensive care. The woman's family claims that failure of the ship's physician to properly treat a heart attack led to an increased risk of a second, fatal heart attack. The two physicians providing care on the ship were trained in Colombia; neither was licensed to practice in the United States, and neither had advanced training in cardiac care.

There is also a case — one of the few involving the death of a cruise ship passenger during an outbreak of gastrointestinal disease — of a 52-year-old man who died while aboard Carnival Cruise Line's *Jubilee* in June 1996. A gastrointestinal virus had struck the ship, afflicting more than 150 passengers and 16 crew members. On the second night Russell Lum complained that he wasn't feeling well; following a bout of nausea, he spent the next day in his cabin. At 1:30 a.m. on the third day, he was transferred to the infirmary and given an intravenous solution to avoid dehydration.

> After a time, the nurse took Lum's blood pressure and said he was improving and could return to his cabin. Tired but relieved, Mrs. Lum hurried to the cabin to get towels and a change of clothes, because her husband had soiled his pants.
>
> "My daughter and niece were awake, and I told them he was fine and would be coming back," Mrs. Lum said. "I was gone about five minutes, and when I got back to the infirmary the doctor and nurse asked me to wait in the waiting room." [After several minutes] ... "they came back and told me that he had taken a turn for the worse and he had died," she said. "I asked them how that was possible, and they said there was nothing they could do."[74]

Russell Lum died as a result of extensive blood loss from a tear in his esophagus caused by vomiting. His family is suing Carnival Cruise Line for his wrongful death. Carnival's lawyer, Curtis Mase, contends that the company was not responsible because the death was an act of God and that Lum had failed to seek timely or appropriate medical care. "'Russell Lum's own negligence contributed to his death and injuries,' Mase said."[75]

To be fair, not all medical emergencies have grave outcomes. These examples represent the worst. What is glaring, however, is that passengers are not normally forewarned about the quality and nature of medical care on cruise ships. Many cruise lines advertise the presence of medical services, but few point out the limited nature of those services. None clearly state that medical services are provided by a concessionaire for whose actions the cruise line has no responsibility or liability. From the cruise line's perspective, medical services are provided as a convenience to passengers.

IS A CRUISE SAFE?

With all of this said, the risk of accidents, attack, and disease onboard a cruise ship is relatively small. Disease and harm are certainly not rampant but there is a degree of risk. Taking simple precautions can reduce many risks, but not all. My avoidance of gastrointestinal illness is in part luck, but in part knowing which foods and beverages are relatively safe and which have a high degree of risk. Can you eliminate all risks? Obviously, the answer is no. The question you must ask is whether the risks present are acceptable.

"SAVE THE WAVES"
— SOUNDS GOOD, BUT ...

IT'S HARD TO FATHOM — a company that projects itself as environmentally responsible being fined $33.5 million for polluting the sea. But it's true. Ever since Royal Caribbean began its "Save the Waves" campaign in 1992, it had continually dumped oil and hazardous chemicals into the environment.

Other cruise lines also project an environmentally friendly image. Princess Cruises has "Planet Princess"; Holland America Line has "Seagoing Environmental Awareness," with the acronym SEA. Royal Caribbean established its Ocean Fund to further promote an image of environmental responsibility.

A perusal of cruise-line brochures and cruise industry websites suggests that the industry is environmentally sustainable and that it always has been environmentally responsible. Press releases and commitments issued by the International Council of Cruise Lines (ICCL) further support this impression, but unfortunately, the reality is quite different.

DOWN THE TOILET AND INTO THE SEA

The US Environmental Protection Agency (EPA) estimates that each passenger generates 100 gallons of wastewater per day, including 10 gallons of sewage.[1] A mega-ship with 5,000 passengers and crew produces almost 500,000 gallons of wastewater and 50,000 gallons of sewage every single day of the year. The sheer volume is mind-boggling.

Cruise ships produce other waste, too. Each passenger, in a single day, accounts for about two pounds of burnable waste (which includes some plastic), one pound of food waste — usually disposed of at sea — and two pounds of glass and tin, which may be disposed of at sea. The International Maritime Organization (IMO) estimates that in sum, each cruise ship passenger produces 7.7 pounds of waste per day. By the end of 2002 the North American cruise industry will accommodate close to 200,000 passengers every day. Add 100,000 crew members, and the volume of waste produced at sea is overwhelming: in one year, more than 50,000 tons of food waste and 100,000 tons each of glass, tin, and burnable waste.

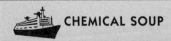 **CHEMICAL SOUP**

Royal Caribbean International estimates that during a seven-day voyage a typical cruise ship generates 141 gallons of photo chemicals, 7 gallons of dry-cleaning waste, 13 gallons of used paints, 5 pounds of batteries, 10 pounds of fluorescent light bulbs, 3 pounds of medical waste, and 108 pounds of expired chemicals.[2]

Add other wastes such as oily bilge water and other engine by-products, fluorescent and mercury vapor lightbulbs, photo-processing chemicals, dry-cleaning waste fluids, print shop waste fluids, photocopier and laser printer toner cartridges, unused and outdated pharmaceuticals, batteries, cardboard and other packing materials, and incinerator ash. The amount produced is not at all well documented, but it must be considerable given the size of most modern ships.

ENVIRONMENTAL RECORD

Royal Caribbean cites three key principles for its Save the Waves program:

(1) reduce the creation or generation of waste material;
(2) recycle as much as possible; and
(3) ensure proper disposal of remaining waste.

It all sounds good, but does it reflects actual practice? The actions of the cruise industry over the past couple of decades have unfortunately fallen short. The result among some is distrust and skepticism about the industry's sincerity about environmental responsibility.

A Brief History

Environmental concern about cruise ships is relatively recent. It was first expressed in the late 1980s, focusing on garbage washing ashore on Florida beaches and along the coast of the Gulf of Mexico. In the early 1990s concern led to surveillance by the US Coast Guard. A number of cruise ships were subsequently charged for illegal disposal of plastic garbage bags and for releasing oil into the sea.

The advent of mega-ships increased concern for the proper disposal of both garbage and sewage. The larger size of cruise ships — an average ship today carries over 2,000 passengers, three times more than an average ship in the 1970s and early 1980s — was accompanied by a growth in the number of cruise ships. The result is exponential increases in the volume of garbage, sewage, and other waste materials. In relatively enclosed areas, such as the Inside Passage in Alaska and British Columbia or parts of the Caribbean, raw sewage has become as big a problem as other discharges from cruise ships.

In 1993, following more than one hundred unsuccessful attempts to have the problem addressed by the state in which offending ships were registered,[3] the American government was forced to take direct action in the form of stricter enforcement for pollution offences.[4]

Princess Cruises was fined $500,000 in April 1993 for dumping more than 20 plastic bags full of garbage off the Florida Keys. Videotape made by a couple on the

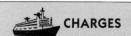 **CHARGES**

Between 1993 and 1998 the US Coast Guard charged cruise ships with 490 safety or environmental violations. In addition, the Coast Guard issued 73 tickets for oil spills of 100 gallons or less.[5]

cruise was used to indict Princess Cruises for unlawful dumping of plastics at sea and was the basis for a plea bargain. Because it is allowed by statute, and as an incentive aimed at encouraging cruise ship passengers to report illegal dumping of waste, the court awarded the couple one-half of the fine. They received $250,000.[6]

Palm Beach Cruises was fined $1 million a year later, after Coast Guard surveillance aircraft videotaped the *Viking Princess* intentionally dumping waste oil, leaving a 2.5-mile-long slick in its wake as it sailed 3.5 miles from the port of Palm Beach. This was the first successful criminal prosecution of the strict new federal oil dumping laws enacted after the *Exxon Valdez* spill. The fine was for both dumping and failing to report the incident.[7]

In the months that followed, Royal Caribbean International was investigated after a report that one of its ships had released oil into the sea. The investigation soon expanded to include two ships in separate incidents. Four years later, Royal Caribbean paid $9 million in fines to settle the cases. In other incidents, Regency Cruises agreed to pay a fine of $250,000 after admitting that two of its ships had dumped garbage-filled plastic bags into Florida waters, and Ulysses Cruises paid a $500,000 fine for two incidents of plastic-wrapped garbage being thrown from the *Seabreeze* off Miami and two cases of dumping oily bilge water. One incident involving garbage had been observed by a musician; the other, by a passenger. Both incidents involving oily bilge water were detected by Coast Guard surveillance.

But it wasn't until 1999 that the issue of pollution from cruise ships came under the spotlight after Royal Caribbean International agreed to pay a record $18-million fine after pleading guilty to numerous pollution-related offences.

> "Royal Caribbean used our nation's waters as its dumping ground, even as it promoted itself as an environmentally 'green' company ... [and] to make matters worse, the company routinely falsified the ships' logs — so much so that its own employees referred to the logs with a Norwegian term meaning fairy tale book....
> [T]his case will sound like a foghorn throughout the maritime industry."[8]
>
> — Attorney General Janet Reno, July 21, 1999

In 1998 Holland America Line paid a $1-million fine and $1 million in restitution following a 1995 incident in which it pumped oily bilge water overboard in Alaska's Inside Passage. The assistant engineer who reported the incident received a reward of $500,000 — again, one-half of the company's fine.

In 2000 the Justice Department subpoenaed records from Norwegian Cruise Line after its parent company, Star Cruises, reported it had uncovered questionable practices prior to its ownership of the company.[13] Carnival Corporation was also sub-poenaed in 2000 for records relating to the environmental prac-tices of ships with each of its six cruise lines.[14] In April 2002 Carnival Corporation pleaded guilty to six counts of falsifying records in relation to oil discharges. In the plea agreement the company admitted to dumping oily waste from five ships operat-ed by Carnival Cruise Line and also admitted that employees had made false entries in record books from 1998 to 2001. Carnival paid a $9-million fine and will contribute $9 million to environ-mental projects over five years. In addition, Carnival agreed to five years of court supervision and also pledged to hire new man-agers and to put in place an executive-level environmental stan-dards program.

In July 2002, Norwegian Cruise Line signed a plea agreement with the US Department of Justice in which it pleaded guilty to the discharge of oily bilge water between 1997 and May 2000, and to falsifying its discharge logs. The company was fined $1 mil-lion and ordered to pay $500,000 toward environmental service projects in South Florida. Federal prosecutors described the sen-tence as lenient.

Trust Us — Let Bygones Be Bygones

There have been some encouraging changes on the part of the industry. Increasingly, the new cruise ships have more efficient engines that use cleaner burning fuels and technologically advanced propulsion systems, such as the Azipod. A large proportion of new ships rely on gas turbine engines and on diesel electric power plants — both are major improvements over the traditional sources of power. However, older ships continue to operate without upgrades.

Money may be a greater motivator than environmental respon-sibility when it comes to moving the cruise industry toward put-ting in place more environmentally friendly practices and tech-nologies. The new podded propulsion systems, such as Azipod and Mermaid, are attractive because they are cost-effective and eliminate a number of main components (long shaft lines, reduc-tion gears, rudders, rudder machinery, transversal stern thrusters), which reduces breakdowns and maintenance costs.[15] These systems also provide fuel savings because of greater hydrodynamic efficien-cy; in addition, they reduce the capital cost of ship construction.

Because it frees space that has traditionally been filled with machinery, another benefit of the Azipod system is that it enables cruise lines to increase the number of revenue-generating cabins onboard a ship. Royal Caribbean CEO Richard Fain suggests that

THE CASE OF ROYAL CARIBBEAN INTERNATIONAL

The case began on October 25, 1994, when the crew of a US Coast Guard tracking plane reported seeing oil slicks off the coast of Puerto Rico. The only ship in the area was the *Sovereign of the Seas*. Coast Guard officials in San Juan were radioed and the ship was investigated when it arrived in port.

The investigation determined that, on at least 5 of its 11 ships, Royal Caribbean International had intentionally bypassed the oily water separator (anti-pollution equipment) so that waste could be discharged directly into the sea. Investigators found that between 1990 and 1994 "on a regular and routine basis, and including at least about one or more times each month," crew members dumped oil-contaminated bilge water overboard. Investigators also found that the company had falsified records that would have documented the releases. Three methods were used for bypassing the oily water separator:

- a connection, concealed beneath the engine-room deck plates, allowed bilge water to be pumped overboard from storage tanks by using the clean bilge system ejector pump
- a pipe which could be routed from the bilge waste tank to the overboard discharge pipe downstream from the oily water separator and through which, using the bilge pump, oil-contaminated bilge waste could be discharged directly overboard
- pumping of bilge wells directly overboard with the ejector pump.

The Coast Guard investigation of the *Sovereign of the Seas* revealed that "at various US ports, mariners allegedly removed the ejector pump bypass system's rubber hose, then closed off the connection the space saving provided by the Azipod system, combined with the use of gas turbine engines on Celebrity Cruises' Millennium-class ships, allows space for up to 50 additional cabins.

between the clean and oily bilge systems with a metal plate to conceal the existence and use of the hose to bypass the oily water separator."[9]

Royal Caribbean was formally charged in December 1996,[10] not for illegal dumping but on a single count of making a false statement to the Coast Guard about the *Nordic Empress* discharge off Bermuda, and a single count for the discharge from the *Sovereign of the Seas* while en route to San Juan. Royal Caribbean paid a $9-million fine in June 1998 to settle cases in San Juan and Miami.[11]

Less than a month later, Royal Caribbean reported a new dumping episode to the US Coast Guard.[12] The offence had been reported to the company by crew members; two engineers were fired.

Based on this episode and dozens of others investigated in other jurisdictions in the United States, Royal Caribbean International pleaded guilty in July 1999 to 21 felony counts of dumping oil and hazardous chemicals and one count of making a false statement to the US Coast Guard. With plea agreements in Miami, New York City, Los Angeles, Anchorage, Puerto Rico, and the US Virgin Islands, the company agreed to pay an $18-million fine. Its violations included dumping not just oil but also dry-cleaning fluids, photographic chemicals, and solvents from the print shop.

In August 1999 the State of Alaska filed suit against Royal Caribbean International alleging seven counts of violating laws on oil and hazardous waste disposal. In January 2000 Royal Caribbean was fined $6.5 million for dumping toxic chemicals and oil-contaminated water into the state's waters. The cruise line agreed not to discharge wastewater within three miles of Alaska's coastline.

Although other, more minor offenses have occurred, no major releases of environmentally hazardous substances have been reported in the past couple of years. In 2000 the State of Alaska instituted a program, called the Alaska Cruise Ship Initiative, initially funded by collected fines, that monitors waste disposal by cruise ships in Alaskan waters, particularly the Inside Passage.

New Water Treatment Systems

New systems for dealing with sewage and "graywater" (water from sinks, showers, and the galley) have also been introduced. One such system, developed by Zenon Environmental of Oakville, Ontario, Canada, filters wastewater and sewage to yield pure water. In view of Alaska's targeted anti-pollution program, the systems are being installed primarily on ships devoted to that market. Holland America Line, for example, clearly states in the Winter 2002 issue of *Mariner* (the company's past passenger magazine), that the Zenon system already has been implemented on two ships; the stated plan was to install the system on three more ships bound for Alaska before the 2002 season.

"Every day a cruise ship generates pollutants that "include as much as 37,000 gallons of oily bilge water; 30,000 gallons of sewage (or black water); 255,000 gallons of non-sewage wastewater from showers, sinks, laundries, baths and galleys (or gray water); 15 gallons of toxic chemicals from photo processing, dry cleaning, and paints; tens of thousands of gallons of ballast water, bearing pathogens and invasive species from foreign ports; seven tons of garbage and solid waste; and air pollution from diesel engines at a level equivalent to thousands of automobiles."[16]

— *The Ocean Conservancy, May 2002*

The incentive is clear. With the new system the company is allowed to dispose of treated wastewater anywhere within the Inside Passage; without the system the ship is required to travel 12 miles from shore before discharging untreated sewage. At the same time, these systems are not being installed on new ships currently being built. It appears that they are being deployed only on ships sailing the Inside Passage of Alaska — only where there is a direct financial benefit for the cruise line. The benefit provided to the environment is questionable. The Zenon system reportedly produces between 30 and 50 tons of sewage sludge per week, which is held until the ship is beyond the twelve mile limit required by MARPOL and then released.

Cruise lines are also being given an incentive by Alaska to clean their smokestack emissions. The state levied $577,500 in fines in 2000 and 2001. Almost one-third of the fines

($175,000) was suspended on the condition that there would be no infractions in 2002. Holland America Line was fined the largest amount: $165,000 for six violations in 2000, of which $55,000 was suspended, and $27,500 for one violation in 2001, which was also suspended. The suspended penalties are conditional on Holland America Line's *Veendam* being without violations in 2002. Similar incentives were provided to Crystal Cruises, Princess Cruises, and World Explorer Cruises, all of which had also polluted the waters.

We Promise to Dump Only What's Legal

In July 1999, several weeks after the plea agreement between the Justice Department and Royal Caribbean Cruise Line, the ICCL made a commitment to standards for waste management, with the assurance that:

> member lines have strengthened their own environmental policies and procedures, and closely monitor onboard activities to ensure these standards are maintained. The internal procedures are designed to meet existing and comprehensive federal, state, and international standards designed to prevent discharges from all commercial vessels.[17]

While the ICCL commitment and mandatory standards set protocols for performance, no one has the responsibility of verifying and enforcing the standards.

Several months after the ICCL commitment, Celebrity Cruises' *Mercury* allegedly dumped perchloroethylene (a dry-cleaning solvent, often called "perc") into San Francisco Bay. After being given a run-around by the EPA, a couple brought the matter to the Bluewater Network, a San Francisco-based environmental group, which is taking legal action. Despite the eyewitness account, Celebrity denied the allegation.[18] The EPA subsequently undertook its own criminal investigation; at this point, the outcome is unknown.

Two years later, in June 2001, the ICCL reaffirmed its commitment by adopting "New Mandatory Environmental Standards for Cruise Ships." The announcement was made while the Alaska State Senate was in a special session considering legislation that would authorize the monitoring of cruise ships emissions and would enforce environmental standards.

The new standards responded to the public outcry against the types of pollution dumped by Royal Caribbean International. However, they were merely consistent with common sense practice and with existing requirements under the International Convention for the Prevention of Pollution from Ships (MARPOL; international regulations for waste disposals at sea). Most of us would think common sense is enough to prevent dumping chemicals such as silver, xylene, benzene, turpentine, methyl ethyl ketone, cadmium, chlorinated hydrocarbons, heavy metals, and perchloroethylene into the sea.

Need for Stricter Regulations

While it is easy to point the finger at the cruise industry as the sole problem, the rules and regulations under which the industry operates is a contributing factor. You may be disgusted by what is thrown into the seas, but in most cases whatever is disposed of is done so legally. Cruise lines act within international guidelines. Under the ICCL commitment, cruise lines have simply agreed to follow those international regulations.

Current Environmental Standards and Initiatives

The primary international regulation of marine pollution is the International Convention for the Prevention of Pollution from Ships (MARPOL).[19] In general terms, MARPOL makes it illegal to dispose of plastic and oil anywhere at sea. Otherwise, almost anything can be legally dumped into the sea.

Two parts of MARPOL apply particularly to cruise ships: [20]

- Annex IV, not yet in force, includes regulations for the prevention of pollution by sewage from ships. It needs ratification by 15 states constituting 50 percent of world tonnage; to date it has been ratified by 75 states constituting 43 percent of world tonnage.
- Annex V, which took effect in 1989, includes regulations for the prevention of pollution by garbage from ships. The annex specifies the Caribbean as a "special area" (a region with stricter regulations than other areas of the ocean); however, that clause will not take effect until onshore garbage disposal facilities are fully available.[21]

INTERNATIONAL CONVENTION FOR THE
PREVENTION OF POLLUTION FROM SHIPS (MARPOL)

Annex IV: Regulations for the Prevention of Pollution by Sewage from Ships
Regulation 8: Discharge of Sewage

(1) [T]he discharge of sewage into the sea is prohibited, except when:

(a) the ship is discharging comminuted and disinfected sewage ... at a distance of more than four nautical miles from the nearest land, or sewage which is not comminuted or disinfected at a distance of more than 12 nautical miles from the nearest land....

[Note that there is no regulation of graywater; in most cases it can be released anywhere.]

Annex V: Regulations for the Prevention of Pollution by Garbage from Ships
Regulation 3: Disposal of Garbage outside Special Areas

(a) The disposal into the sea of all plastics, including but not limited to synthetic ropes, synthetic fishing nets and plastic garbage bags is prohibited;

(b) The disposal into the sea of the following garbage shall be made as far as practical from the nearest land but in any case is prohibited if the distance from the nearest land is less than:

i. 25 nautical miles for dunnage [material placed between cargo to prevent shifting], lining, and packing material which will float;

ii. 12 nautical miles for food wastes and all other garbage including paper products, rags, glass, metal, bottles, crockery, and similar refuse.

(c) Disposal into the sea of garbage specified in subparagraph (b) (ii) of this regulation may be permitted when it is passed through a comminuter or grinder and made as far as practical from the nearest land but in any case is prohibited if the distance from the nearest land is less than three nautical miles. Such comminuted or ground garbage shall be capable of passing through a screen with openings no greater than 25 mm.[22]

Beyond 12 miles of a coastline there is very little, other than plastic and oil, that cannot legally be dumped at sea. Even within 3 or 4 miles of the coast, much can be disposed of overboard, so long as it has been ground up to fit through a one-inch screen.

Despite the shortcoming of international regulations, most of us living in North America assume that federal and local laws protect the coastal environment. A report prepared in March 2000 by the Bluewater Network's Cruise Ship Campaign suggests this is not the case.[23] The fact is that American law has many loopholes and gaps related to discharges from cruise ships. Many types of discharges from cruise ships are exempt from key regulations under the US Clean Water Act.

For example, the Clean Water Act makes it unlawful to discharge any pollutant from a point source into American waters unless a permit is obtained under the National Pollutant Discharge Elimination System (NPDES), but cruise ships are exempt. The act specifically provides that discharges of sewage from vessels, effluent from properly functioning marine engines, laundry, shower, and galley sink wastes (graywater), or any other discharge "incidental to the normal operation of the vessel" are exempt from the requirement to obtain NPDES permits. Even though the EPA has found that graywater has the potential to cause harmful environmental effects, the Clean Water Act permits it to be legally dumped anywhere except the Great Lakes and certain parts of Alaska's Inside Passage.

 **WASTE-AWAY!**

In the year 2000 cruise ships in Alaska produced 32 million pounds of waste, a 40-percent increase from 1995. Also that year, pollution from cruise ships in the Caribbean increased by 41 percent to 165 million pounds of waste and in the Mediterranean, by 80 percent to 48 million pounds.[24]

THE QUESTION OF ENVIRONMENTAL SUSTAINABILITY

With as many as 25 ships sailing the Inside Passage at any point in time, and with an average of 2,000 passengers per ship, on a given day the area can hold 50,000 people producing 5 million gallons of wastewater, including 500,000 gallons of sewage. In addition, those 50,000 people would produce 27.5 tons of food waste and 55 tons of glass and tin. And all of this can be legally disposed of at sea.

Two issues exist. One, there is an issue of principle: quite simply, that cruise ships should not be permitted to release environmentally harmful discharges into coastal waters. The risks associated with each type of waste being released must be considered.[25] And two, there is the issue of sheer volume. Communities along the Inside Passage in British Columbia and Alaska have a huge amount of pollution introduced into their coastal waters and into the food chain.

A cruise ship produces various types of waste.[26] The nature of each type of waste and the laws that apply are worth mentioning. While I will focus on American laws and regulations, in almost every case these laws are as strict as or stricter than Canadian laws and regulations. The main exception is that, as of January 1, 2001, Canadian law prohibits the discharge of sewage in ten marine sites within the Strait of Georgia, and it also prohibits disposal of garbage in the Inside Passage within Canadian waters.[27]

Sewage

One of the more troubling pollutants produced by a cruise ship is sewage. It contributes to the degradation of the marine environment by introducing disease-causing microorganisms and excessive nutrients. Shellfish and other filter feeders may pick up sewage released in the vicinity of shellfish beds. Pathogens can become concentrated in their tissues, making them unsafe for human consumption. Sewage-borne pathogens are also harmful to corals. Nutrients such as nitrogen and phosphorous, also found in sewage, promote excessive algal growth which in turn consumes oxygen in the water and kills fish.

Although sewage is defined as a pollutant under the Clean Water

 **EFFLUENT**

The Environmental Protection Agency (EPA) estimates that a cruise ship produces 10 gallons of sewage per passenger, per day. The environmental effect is significant, given that sewage produced on a cruise ship is more concentrated than domestic sewage because cruise ships use less water volume for toilets than would be normal onshore.

Act, sewage from cruise ships is exempt. The Clean Water Act prohibits generally the dumping of untreated or inadequately treated sewage within three miles of shore. But beyond that, it's legal for a cruise ship to empty its toilets into the sea.

Most cruise ships attempt to deal with the problem of sewage through the use of a "marine sanitation device" — an onboard sewage treatment plant. If operating properly, sewage treated by a marine sanitation device will not exceed a fecal coliform count of 200 per 100 milliliters of water, nor contain suspended solids greater than 150 milligrams per liter of water. Monitoring done by the State of Alaska during the summer of 2000, however, indicated actual rates of fecal coliform and suspended solids as much as 100,000 times greater than allowed.

While marine sanitation devices are intermittently inspected by the Coast Guard to ensure they work properly, the cruise ship is not held to the same standards as industries and municipalities that discharge treated sewage into state waters. The latter are required to sample, monitor, and report on levels of pollutants and other parameters of effluents discharged. Cruise ships have no such requirements.

Graywater

Detergents, cleaners, oil and grease, metals, pesticides, medical and dental waste — all of this can be found in graywater. It includes whatever passengers put down their drains, any runoff from food preparation (including the washing of produce, which may possess pesticide or other chemical residue), the laundry, the washing of dishes and utensils, and anything else that goes down the drain. Graywater has the potential to cause adverse environmental effects, according to a study of discharges from vessels of the US Armed Forces.[28]

Until recently the Great Lakes was the only area with explicit regulations controlling the release of graywater in American or Canadian waters. US federal legislation passed in December 2000 extended protection to specific coastal areas of Alaska's Inside Passage.[29] However, even though the American delegation to the Marine Environment Protection Committee of the International Maritime Organization (IMO) suggested in December 1999 that graywater may contain contaminants which pose greater threats than sewage discharges, and recommended that some form of regulation be put into place, the government has taken no action beyond the limited protection within a small area of Alaska's Inside Passage.

Hazardous Wastes

Until the Royal Caribbean legal cases proved otherwise, most people would have assumed that hazardous wastes would not be dumped into the ocean. Now we know that not only do cruise ships produce hazardous wastes, they might very well release them into the ocean. That is why the ICCL guidelines include prohibitions against such things as:

- dry-cleaning sludge (which contains perchloroethylene, known to cause cancer and birth defects in humans, and in small amounts to be toxic to aquatic animals)
- waste from photo processing and X-ray development (which contains silver, a toxic waste)
- paint waste and dirty solvents (which contain toluene, xylene, benzene, turpentine, methyl ethyl ketone, to name a few)
- print shop wastes (which contains hydrocarbons, chlorinated hydrocarbons, and heavy metals)
- fluorescent light bulbs (which contain mercury)
- batteries (which contain lead, corrosives, and cadmium).

That a cruise line would dump these chemicals into the ocean is one thing. That there are no clear regulations applying to the management and disposal of these wastes is even more frightening.

There are two basic problems with existing regulations. First, the EPA holds the view that regulations on disposal of hazardous waste apply to cruise ships when the waste has been landed on shore, but do not apply to ships at sea, even when a ship is in American waters.

Second, there is a question as to which regulations apply to cruise ships. Is a cruise ship a "small quantity generator" — producing less than 2,200 pounds of hazardous waste per month — or a "large quantity generator" — producing more than that amount? A small quantity generator is subject to less stringent record keeping and reporting than a large quantity generator. In

ACCORDING TO OUR LOGS ...

Even with international guidelines and the ICCL's commitment, it appears that dangerous chemicals are still being released. In October 2001 I took a transatlantic cruise aboard the *Seabourn Goddess I*. One day, midway through the crossing, passengers watched as a fluorescent green stream of liquid was twice released from the back of the ship. Many took pictures, and the matter was a topic of much discussion. A number of passengers asked the chief engineer about the emission. He explained that it was a chemical used to detect leaks and that it was legal to release it at sea. However, his comments contradicted the MARPOL log on the bridge that listed the emission as food waste, and were inconsistent with an explanation given by an officer who said the chemicals should have been put into a holding tank until they reached shore.

There was no way to know which account was correct, but in any event, both explanations were inconsistent with what was recorded in the official record. If I had complained to the Federal Maritime Commission or the US Coast Guard, the matter would likely have to be referred to the country under whose flag the ship sailed. Upon returning home, I relayed my concerns to a representative of Seabourn's chief executive officer. He demonstrated no real interest or concern.

determining which category a ship falls into, is each ship taken as an independent entity or is the cruise line taken as a whole?

Clarification on these sorts of issues is one of the agenda items of the Bluewater Network's Cruise Ship Campaign. Unsurprisingly, the cruise industry has actively opposed their efforts, arguing that ICCL guidelines are enough. Environmentalists argue that there is no basis for confidence that the guidelines are sufficient.

Solid Waste

A cruise ship also produces a large volume of nonhazardous solid waste. This includes huge amounts of plastic, paper, wood, cardboard, food waste, cans, and glass. In a typical week a Holland America ship with 1,200 passengers generates an estimated eight tons of garbage — much of which is incinerated at sea with the ash discharged into the water.[30] Some of the garbage is held onboard and landed ashore for either recycling or disposal.

American law prohibits the discharge of all garbage within 3 miles of shore. It also prohibits certain types of garbage from being dumped between 3 and 25 miles, and the discharge of plastics anywhere at sea. While the dumping of plastic — particularly garbage-filled plastic bags — was a problem in the early and mid-1990s, enforcement appears to have effectively stopped the practice.

Oily Bilge Water

According to Royal Caribbean's 1998 environmental report, a typical cruise ship on a one-week voyage generates an estimated 25,000 gallons of oily bilge water. This water collects in the bottom of a vessel's hull from condensation, water-lubricated shaft seals, propulsion system cooling, and other engine room sources. It contains fuel, oil, and wastewater from engines and other machinery, and may also include solid wastes such as rags, metal shavings, paint, glass, and cleaning agents.

The Clean Water Act, as amended by the Oil Pollution Act, regulates disposal of oily bilge water in American waters. The act prohibits the discharge of oil or hazardous substances "in such quantities as may be harmful" within 200 miles of the coast. The quantity needed to be "harmful" is not defined, which leaves open the question of whether current regulations are enough. The Clean Water Act allows discharge of oil within 12 miles of shore as long as it has passed through a 15-parts-per-million oily water separator and does not cause a visible sheen.[31]

 WHY WOULD THEY DUMP OIL AT SEA?

One possible reason why cruise ships circumvent the oily water separator and dump oil overboard is that doing so saves money. The membranes for the oily water separator can cost as much as $80,000 per year. In addition, disposing of the waste from the oily water separator ashore can cost another $300,000 per year. By eliminating these costs, a ship's officers could receive larger end-of-the-year bonuses for staying under budget.[32] That end-of-the-year bonus is the incentive for officers; however, the successful prosecution of Royal Caribbean and Holland America, and the hefty fines, may be an effective incentive for cruise lines to stop such practices.

Beyond 12 miles, oil or oily mixtures may be discharged while proceeding en route and if the oil content of the effluent without dilution is less than 100 parts per million.

Oil and other elements in bilge water pose great risks to fish and other marine organisms. Even in minute concentrations, oil can kill fish or have numerous sublethal (not deadly, but close) effects such as changes in heart and respiratory rates, enlarged livers, reduced growth, fin erosion, and various biochemical and cellular changes. Oil causes skin and eye lesions in marine mammals and interferes with swimming ability. If ingested, oil can cause gastrointestinal tract hemorrhaging, renal failure, liver toxicity, and blood disorders. Research indicates that by-products from the biological breakdown of petroleum products can harm fish and wildlife, as well as threaten human health if these fish or other creatures are eaten.

The Case of Orcas in the Inside Passage

The problem of pollution from ships has reached crisis proportions. It isn't only cruise ships, but they are part of the problem.

In July 2001 the *Anchorage Daily News* printed a story focusing on the poisoning of orcas (killer whales) from contaminants, suggesting that the problem of industrial pollutants is worldwide and that the contaminants have infiltrated Alaska's food chain.[33] High levels of pollutants have been documented in a wide range of animals, including sea otters, seals, walruses, peregrine falcons, northern fur seals, and bald eagles. As the chemicals move up the food chain, they concentrate and build up in fatty tissues.[34]

The highest concentration of contaminants appears among orcas known as "transients" (those which roam over a large area, as opposed to "resident" orcas which remain within a smaller home range) and which feed primarily on marine mammals. Among ten orcas sampled in 1999 and 2000, several transients appeared to be among the most contaminated marine mammals ever measured. One

 **ORCAS**

There are now 20 percent fewer orcas living around the southern end of Vancouver Island, British Columbia. In 1995 there were 99 resident whales; by 2001 the resident population had dropped to 78.[35]

whale had PCBs at 370 parts per million and DDT at about 470 parts per million. Another had PCBs at 651 parts per million and DDT at 1,003 parts per million. To put this into context, the US Food and Drug Administration's standard for human consumption of fish is 2 parts per million of PCBs and 5 parts per million of DDT.[36]

While the cruise industry is not a source of DDT and PCBs, this illustration demonstrates the fragility of the marine environment, and underlines the importance of control over disposal of chemicals and other pollutants at sea.

Environmental Challenges

The potential for environmental damage through pollution by the cruise industry is great. There have been some moves to attempt to improve control and regulation of the industry, and these have had moderately positive effects, but overall the laws and regulations remain lax. With the cruise industry's exponential growth, the environment is losing out to a far greater extent than any gains made through modest improvements.

History has demonstrated that environmental responsibility has not been voluntarily assumed. Most industry innovations and initiatives have followed a pattern: deny that their behavior is a problem, lobby government to not impose regulations, resist enforcement, and, after being caught, announce new regulations or commitments. Alaska provides a good case in point.

DESTINATION: ALASKA

In many ways, Alaska is unique in its relationship with the cruise industry. The state attracts a large number of cruise ships during the season from May through September. During these five months in 2001, more than 680,000 passengers visited Alaska — a 170-percent increase from 1990.

In total, more tourists arrive to Alaska by cruise ship from May through September than there are year-round residents in the entire state. One journalist observed that cruise ships, with roughly 45,000

 **INVASION**

More than 87 percent of tourists visiting Juneau in 2001 arrived by cruise ship.

passengers aboard on a typical Alaska day, constitute the third largest city in the state. No doubt, the cruise industry is a major source of income to the Alaskan economy.

The natural beauty and resources that attract visitors to Alaska are an incentive to the state government to protect the environment, as is reflected in the strong steps that have been taken to monitor and regulate the cruise industry. In July 2001 Alaska became the first state to regulate water and air pollution from cruise ships. Although generally resisted by the industry, these steps have not resulted in fewer cruise visits to the area. To the contrary, steady increases continue.

En Route to Regulation

Broad-based concerns about pollution from cruise ships arose after Holland America Line in 1998 and Royal Caribbean International pled guilty in 1999 to criminal charges of dumping oily wastes and other hazardous chemicals in the Inside Passage. In addition to the federal fines paid by both companies, Royal Caribbean had a $3.5-million fine levied in January 2000 in state court.[37]

Although there had been previous oil spills in and around Glacier Bay, some resulting from accidents at sea, the public outcry was relatively limited. The cases involving Holland America and Royal Caribbean, however, had not just one but three separate effects.

You Are Not Entirely Welcome Here

The first effect was that some Alaskan communities decided to limit cruise ship visits. Residents of Sitka, for example, overwhelmingly voted down a proposal to construct a wharf that would enable cruise ships to offload passengers directly into the downtown area. The town of 8,800 people believed that the need to transport passengers from the ship to the port using lifeboats (known as "tenders") would keep a lid on its more than 225,000 cruise passenger visits per year.

The town of Tenakee Springs was more aggressive with its proclamation that cruise ship tourism is incompatible with the community's lifestyle, facilities, and services. Tenakee Springs vowed to take whatever steps necessary to prevent that type of tourism. When the first cruise ship arrived in August 1998 — a small ship with only 120 passengers — the town tried to persuade the ship to cancel the visit. After that effort failed, citizens handed leaflets to cruise passengers as they disembarked, telling them that although they were unwelcome as part of a large organized tour, they would be welcome to return on their own. Most businesses closed during the visit.[38]

Public Support for Increased Taxes

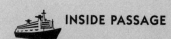

INSIDE PASSAGE

In a one-week trip, a typical cruise ship generates about 210,000 gallons of sewage. During peak summer season, with an average of 20 ships each carrying 2,000 passengers, the daily discharge of sewage in the Inside Passage is approximately 2.5 million gallons per day, equivalent to the entire amount of sewage discharged in the city of Juneau.[39]

The second effect was that the publicity around cruise ship pollution tipped the balance in favor of new taxes on cruise ship passengers. In 1999 voters in Juneau approved, with a 70-percent majority, a $5 head tax for each cruise passenger landing in the city.[40] A similar tax had been defeated just three years earlier. The $5 head tax was the first time any port of call in an American state had imposed such a fee.[41]

The town of Haines followed suit with a 4-percent sales tax on shore excursions and onshore purchases. Many journalists suggested that the effort backfired when Royal Caribbean canceled future stops at the port. However, the reason for the cancellations was purely economic: its plea agreement with the US government had disbarred Royal Caribbean, meaning that it could not enter into contracts with the federal government for five years. As such, it is effectively banned from Glacier Bay National Park. It goes to Hubbard Bay instead, which requires traveling farther. To visit Skagway (a financially lucrative stop), Hubbard Bay, and Haines, ships have to travel at higher speeds, which results in higher fuel costs. The income generated by stopping at Haines would not offset this additional expense.

In 2001 the town of Skagway considered imposing a higher sales tax during the summer months, but the initiative was defeated in city council. A citizen group called Responsible Cruising in Alaska tried to have an initiative placed on the 2002 statewide ballot to charge a head tax of $50 to $75 on cruise ship passengers, along with a corporate income tax and a 33-percent tax on onboard gambling. The initiative was put on hold in late 2001.

Shortly after, Alaska senator Rick Halford and Governor Tony Knowles individually proposed schemes for a head tax on all cruise passengers entering the state.[42] In February 2002 the governor formally proposed to the state legislature a cruise passenger tax of $30 per head. A related story in a cruise industry trade publication indicated that there were "some assertions that the head tax is unconstitutional. In the event the head tax is struck down, his [Knowles's] bill includes a provision that would instead levy a corporate income tax on the cruise industry."[43] The governor's bill was sent to the Senate Transportation Committee but went no further during the 2002 legislative season.

Public Support for Monitoring and Enforcement

The third major effect of the Holland America and Royal Caribbean cases was an increased interest in monitoring cruise ships, not just for oil pollution but also for sewage disposal and air pollution. The state Department of Environmental Conservation and the US Coast Guard launched a joint cruise ship initiative in December 1999.

The initiative began with meetings between the state, the Coast Guard, the EPA, members of the cruise industry, and representatives from environmental groups. The goal was to discuss the activities and operations of cruise ships and assess possible environmental issues. When the work groups realized there was little technical data to support cruise industry claims, they developed a scheme for sampling wastewater from the ships and for monitoring air emis-

> "Of the 36 samples of sewage required by federal law to be treated, not one fully complied with federal standards.... Even more alarming, more than 70 percent of the gray water samples had levels of fecal coliform bacteria — an indication of human waste — that far exceeded the standards imposed on sewage."[44]
>
> — *Alaska Governor Tony Knowles, October 6, 2000*

sions. The cruise lines' participation in the scheme was voluntary. Thirteen of 24 ships refused to participate, choosing to go beyond the 12-mile legal boundary to dump raw sewage without monitoring and without limitations.

The results of monitoring during the summer of 2000 were, in the words of Alaska's governor, "disgusting and disgraceful." Seventy-nine of 80 ships' effluent had levels of fecal coliform or total suspended solids that would be illegal on land — up to 100,000 times the federal standard. This was true of both blackwater (waste from toilets) and graywater.[45] As well, all samples indicated that "conventional pollutants" were part of the wastewater. According to the Juneau port commander for the Coast Guard, the results were so extreme that it might be necessary to consider possible design flaws and capacity issues with the Coast Guard-approved sewage treatment systems.[46]

The results of air-emission monitoring of air emissions were not impressive. The EPA had cited six cruise ship companies (involving 13 ships) for air pollution violations during the 1999 season, and in 2000 the situation had not improved. In August 2000 state investigators charged seven companies — Holland America Line, Princess Cruises, Celebrity Cruises, Norwegian Cruise Line, Carnival Cruise Line, World Explorer Cruise Line, and Crystal Cruises — for 11 violations of state smoke-opacity standards while their ships were docked at Juneau between mid-July and mid-August.

In a bid to repair its image, Princess Cruises announced in September 2000 that its ships would plug into Juneau's power supply while in port instead of running their smoke-belching engines to generate electricity. The initiative, which required an investment of $4.5 million by the cruise line and $300,000 by the city, began in July 2001.

The Federal Government Responds

The initiative's monitoring results led to Alaska's Senator Frank Murkowski introducing federal legislation that regulated the dumping of raw sewage in a specific area of the Inside Passage: the Alexander Archipelago, including within the Kachemak Bay National Estuarine Research Reserve. Passed in December 2000, the cruise ship operations bill extends protection to "doughnut holes" (defined by the state Department of Environmental Conservation as "small areas of the ocean within the Inside Passage that are more than three miles from the Alaska mainland and any islands") where such disposal was common; these areas had previously been treated as being outside federal waters.[47] The legislation also set standards for treated sewage and banned all discharges while ships were within one mile of shore.[48]

The Alaska Cruise Ship Initiative

Based on the results of the summer 2000 monitoring, in March 2001 Governor Knowles introduced legislation designed to strengthen state monitoring of the cruise industry's waste disposal practices. Passed two months later, the legislation enforces state clean air and water standards for cruise ships, and also sets forth a fee of $1 per passenger to pay for pollution monitoring programs, inspections, and enforcement by state officials.

House Bill 260 (Commercial Passenger Vessel Regulation and Fees) passed Alaska's House of Representatives on May 3, 2001, with a vote of 35 to three. However, it got held up by the senate's transportation committee, where the chairperson not only warned that the act would not pass his committee before the session was adjourned, but also claimed that the measure was unfair because it would require smaller vessels to meet the same environmental standards as large cruise ships.

Five days later, after the legislature had adjourned for the summer, the governor called a special session for the bill to be properly considered. The special session began one month later and the bill was passed on June 20. It was signed by the governor on June 29 and took effect July 1, 2001.

Although the state law was not more stringent than existing federal law regarding the disposal of sewage or pollution from smokestack emissions, it provided three things:

1. a verified program of sampling, testing, and reporting of wastewater and air discharges
2. enforceable standards for what cruise ships may discharge in Alaska waters
3. a requirement that the cruise ship industry pay the costs of the program.

ALASKA CRUISE SHIP INITIATIVE

COMMERCIAL PASSENGER VESSEL ENVIRONMENTAL COMPLIANCE PROGRAM

Wastewater Discharge Standards

- **Untreated Sewage:** Passenger vessels are prohibited from discharging untreated sewage, i.e. sewage that has not met all applicable federal processing standards and effluent limitation standards. This means that sewage must be processed through a properly operated and maintained marine sanitation device and meet the applicable effluent standards.
- **Treated Sewage:** Sewage cannot be discharged if it has suspended solids greater than 150 milligrams per liter or a fecal coliform count greater than 200 colonies per 100 milliliters. Small vessels can delay compliance upon submission of a plan that provides interim protective measures.
- **Graywater:** Graywater cannot be discharged if it has suspended solids greater than 150 milligrams per liter or a fecal coliform count greater than 200 colonies per 100 milliliters. Vessels can delay compliance upon submission of an interim plan.
- **DEC [Department of Environmental Conservation]** can establish numeric and narrative standards by regulation for any other parameters for treated sewage and graywater, including chlorine, chemical oxygen demand, and biological oxygen demand.

Restrictions on Discharges

Large vessels may not discharge treated sewage or graywater unless the vessel is proceeding at a speed of not less than six knots and more than one nautical mile from shore, complies with effluent standards, and is not in a no-discharge zone. Small vessels are not subject to this provision. Large passenger vessels are excused from compliance if the discharges are proven to meet strict secondary treatment standards.[49]

Alaska became the first state with the authority to inspect ships and prosecute violators, and to regulate air pollution, trash disposal, and handling of hazardous waste and sewage. As such, Alaska's Environmental Compliance Program reflects a basic lack of trust in the cruise industry's respect for environmental regulations.

This lack of trust was reinforced even while the bill was still under consideration. In the first five weeks of the 2001 Alaska cruise season, four cruise ships were cited for violations of the US Clean Water Act.

- On May 5, 2001, the *Norwegian Sky* discharged treated sewage in the Alexander Archipelago. Tests of the effluent showed a fecal coliform count 3,500 times the allowable federal standard and suspended solids 180 times the standard.[50]

- A week later, on May 12, 2001, Holland America Line's *Westerdam* accidentally discharged graywater while docked at Juneau. A valve that failed to close completely allowed about 100 gallons to flow into the harbor. A passerby who noticed an odd color and odor in the water reported the incident to the Coast Guard.

- On June 6, 2001, Celebrity Cruises' *Mercury* was charged with discharging treated wastewater at Juneau. Although the ship had cutting-edge technology for treatment of wastewater, it hadn't yet received approval to discharge in protected areas. Tests of the wastewater indicated that it was more acidic than permitted for discharging within a mile from shore.[51]

- On June 18, 2001, Royal Caribbean's *Rhapsody of the Seas* illegally discharged 200 gallons of graywater into Juneau's harbor while wastewater was being transferred to a holding tank. But the holding tank was full, so wastewater was released through an overboard discharge valve. The *Juneau Empire*, in its report of the incident, quotes Nancy Wheatley, a senior vice-president for Royal Caribbean, as stating: "they were using too many pumps, pumping it too fast, and they didn't shut the pumps off quite fast enough. They got essentially a splash of gray water out the air vent.... It should not have happened and we're sorry it did."[52]

Monitoring had been ongoing on a voluntary basis before the legislation passed into law; it increased after July 1. For an indication of the results reported by the Alaska Department of Environmental Conservation at the end of the summer 2001, see the textbox entitled "Interim Cruise Ship Sampling Data Summary" (page 110).

Glacier Bay

A second issue of interest to Alaskans, and to others living outside the state, is the preservation of Glacier Bay National Park. Although the park is under federal jurisdiction, it is within Alaska's boundaries and reflects the state's environmental politics. The main issue relates to the number of cruise ships permitted to enter Glacier Bay.

Glacier Bay became a hot environmental issue in 1994. Late that year, Congressman Don Young and Senator Murkowski pressured the Department of the Interior to increase the number of cruise ships allowed per year in Glacier Bay National Park by more than 70 percent, from 107 to 184.[54] Each politician was assuming the chairpersonship for the committee that had jurisdiction over most agencies and programs of the Department of the Interior. From that position, they instructed the Secretary of the Interior to direct the National Park Service to change the vessel management part of its plan to allow 184 visits per year — an average of two visits per day during the 92-day season.[55]

Environmentalists and the park service's own experts opposed the increase in the number of permits, citing concern for the abundant wildlife in the park — including several species of whales, Stellar sea lions, seals, and otters — as the mouth of the bay is a major feeding area. Following a sharp decline in the number of humpback whales in the bay, in 1978 strict speed limits had been imposed on cruise ships, and the number of entry permits issued for the park was reduced by 20 percent. Between 1982 and 1991, this reduction was slowly rolled back.

Under pressure to increase ship entries, the park service solicited public comments. Eighty-five percent of respondents favored fewer rather more permits. Consequently, the Alaska politicians were unsuccessful in forcing the number of permits to 184, but the limit was raised to 139 for the peak months of June, July, and August. (Visits during May and September are not included in the quota.) The new limits took effect in 1996.

In response to the decision, in 1997 the National Parks Conservation Association sued the Park Service. In February 2001 the ninth circuit court of appeals found that the Park Service had erred when it responded to industry appeals by allowing a 30-

INTERIM CRUISE SHIP SAMPLING DATA SUMMARY

**ALASKA DEPARTMENT OF ENVIRONMENTAL CONSERVATION
DIVISION OF AIR AND WATER QUALITY
SEPTEMBER 6, 2001**

Summary of Results

- Preliminary 2001 ambient air monitoring data collected in downtown Juneau area through late July 2001 show that the maximum levels measured for three pollutants of concern — sulfur dioxide (SO_2), oxides of nitrogen (NO_x), and particulates that are 2.5 micron in size or smaller ($PM_{2.5}$) — are well below state and federal allowable limits.

- A total of 238 smokestack opacity readings have been taken in Juneau, Skagway and Haines from the start of the cruise season in May through August 28, 2001. Nineteen are currently under review for potential violations of the marine vessel visible air emission opacity standards. Last year there were 30 alleged violations for opacity violations and 2 alleged violations for air pollution violations.

- Six of the seven ships for which wastewater sampling results are summarized are discharging graywater within Alaska waters; only one is discharging blackwater in Alaska waters. One vessel is discharging both gray- and blackwater outside Alaska waters. The samples are for conventional pollutants only. Difficulty in transporting samples from ships to the laboratory in a timely manner resulted in nearly 50 percent of the fecal coliform samples being invalidated. Some ships are being resampled for fecal coliform.

- Overall, the wastewater samples show variable pollutant levels, e.g.,
  — chlorine residual ranges from non-detectable to 70 mg/l (Water Quality standard 0.002 mg/l)
  — fecal coliform bacteria: 19 to 9,000,000 per 100 ml (HB 260 limit 200/100 ml)
  — pH: 4 to 10 (Water Quality standard 6.5 to 8.5)

— and total suspended solids: 18 to 26,000 mg/l (HB 260 limit 150 mg/l)

- While they are not subject to enforcement action, some results for fecal coliform bacteria and total suspended solids from samples taken prior to the effective date of HB 260 exceed the state's new effluent limits.

- There also are wastewater sample results that exceed Alaska's water quality standards for residual chlorine or pH. However, it is important to recognize that effluent limits only apply to fecal coliform bacteria and total suspended solids and water quality criteria are not directly applicable to the concentration of a pollutant in a holding tank, wastewater stream or effluent.

(...)

- One wastewater sample data set taken from a discharge line, of two collected after the July 1, 2001 effective date of the new state law, shows a total suspended solids of 189 mg/l, above the effluent standard of 150 mg/l. Both post-July 1 samples were well below the state's fecal coliform effluent standard of 200 colonies/100 ml under the new law. The one sample is under review by ADEC [Alaska Department of Environmental Conservation] for consideration of a TSS [total suspended solids] violation.

- The cruise industry has introduced some procedures for stack emission reduction, including: gas turbine engines, enhanced combustion technology, and shore-side power hook-ups.

- The industry continues to evaluate, test and bring on-line new technology for advanced wastewater treatment. The USCG [US Coast Guard] has approved two ships for wastewater discharge anywhere in Alaska (except specifically prohibited areas) this season, including in-port. These ships have achieved very low fecal coliform, TSS, biochemical oxygen demand (BOD) and chlorine sample results, through installation of state-of-the-art treatment technology.[53]

[*HB260 = House Bill 260: Commercial Passenger Vessel Regulation and Fees] percent increase in summer cruise ship traffic in Glacier Bay without doing a full study of the environmental impact the additional ships would have. The government appealed the decision. US district court judge James Singleton upheld it in August 2001, ordering an immediate reduction in the number of ships allowed into Glacier Bay National Park.

Senator Ted Stevens sought to override the court decision with a rider to the appropriations bill for the Department of the Interior. The rider instructed the National Park Service to freeze cruise ship entries at the current level of 139 ships until it completed an environmental impact statement as had been ordered by the court in February.[56] The rider passed the Senate in August but didn't pass the House early enough to take effect in 2001. It did take effect in 2002.

Senator Stevens' position — that conservationists needed to prove allegations of adverse impacts on the park — was temporarily undermined by discovery of a dead pregnant female humpback whale floating very near the entrance to Glacier Bay on July 16, 2001. The whale, first observed in 1979 and followed for 22 years, was known as Whale Number 68. An autopsy indicated that the death was most probably the result of a collision with a cruise ship, a conclusion confirmed a month later. Tips from passengers suggest that the whale and Princess Cruises' *Dawn Princess* had collided.[57]

The incident gave increased credence to claims by the National Parks Conservation Association. However, it appears that environmental decisions are so politicized that the support may not change government policies. This politicization is reflected by contributions to the Alaska Republican party of $25,000 each from Holland America Line, Princess Cruises, and Royal Caribbean International. Within one month of a federal judge's ruling in June 2001 that struck down major sections of Alaska's campaign finance law and which legalized so-called soft money contributions, the Republican party had received $90,000 in corporate donations; in contrast, the Democratic party had received $5,000.[58]

DESTINATION: THE CARIBBEAN

Environmental concerns among Caribbean countries have had less success than Alaska. As in Juneau, these concerns have been reflected in efforts to raise the head tax charged for each passenger. But in the Caribbean, the situation is a bit different.

Increased Port Charges to Pay for Garbage Disposal

Caribbean ports made several efforts to increase their port charges in the early 1990s. In most cases, these increases were intended to increase revenue. For example, in 1992 the seven-member Organization of Eastern Caribbean States (OECS) raised port fees from $3.00 to a uniform $9.25 per visitor, but pressure from the cruise industry forced them to roll the fees back to their original level.[59] They raised them to $10 per visitor in 1995 and again were forced to roll them back. After bowing to pressure in 1992 when it raised port charges and faced threats of boycott,[60] the Bahamas successfully resisted pressure from cruise lines to lower its new $15 head tax in 1994.[61] In 1993 Jamaica gave into pressure, reduced its tax, and agreed to phase in an increase over four years.[62] As a means of persuasion, cruise lines used the credible threat of moving their ships to another port.

Disputes over port fees resumed in 1997 after six Caribbean islands — Antigua, Dominica, Grenada, St. Kitts, St. Lucia, and St. Vincent (all OECS members) — announced that, effective December 1, they would begin charging every cruise ship passenger an additional $1.50 head tax. Unlike earlier efforts, the extra cash in this case was earmarked to defray the cost of improving waste management systems at the islands. They were participating in a region-wide program of waste disposal based in Port of Spain, Trinidad, sponsored by the International Maritime Organization and financed by the World Bank. The entire program across the region was expected to cost $54 million.

Implementation of MARPOL's designation of the Caribbean as a "special area" depends on construction of the waste management system. There is perverse incentive for the cruise industry to oppose the taxes needed to fund its operation; as long as construction is delayed, Annex V will not take effect.

After almost a year, cruise lines withdrew their opposition to the new tax in April 1998, following intervention by the World Bank. The bank explained that the island governments had no choice in the matter — they had signed on with the waste disposal project, and collecting the tax from each visitor was part of the agreement. The agreement provided that the World Bank would finance new landfills for each nation, provided that the new tax revenues were used to run the landfills.

Although Carnival Cruise Line had opposed the tax, in March 1998 it agreed to accept the additional $1.50 in the case of Grenada in order to help the country deal with its garbage problem. Carnival's vice-president of public relations, Tim Gallagher, indicated that the cruise line still viewed the new tax as unfair and a dangerous precedent for a company that disposes of most of its solid waste aboard its modern fleet. He said that Carnival had yet to decide whether to pay the tax in the other five nations. "We do not mind paying for something if it's a service being provided for us," he said. "But we do not want to pay for facilities we don't use."[63]

Further insight into the company's attitude is reflected in Gallagher's concession that $1.50 a head — on top of the current $3 arrival tax, the lowest in the region — seems paltry. But, he stressed, "The reason that Carnival Corp. makes the kind of money we do is because we pay great, great attention to controlling our costs. Sure it's just $1.50. But it's $1.50 here, then $1.50 there, then $1.50 over there. When you allow people to unfairly charge for things, then you open a Pandora's box."[64]

In November 1999 Carnival Cruise Line reversed its decision and announced that it would again boycott Grenada over the tax.[65] The resulting confrontation remains a stalemate.

At the same time, the problem of pollution in the Caribbean region continues. It isn't just solid waste, which Carnival Cruise Lines says it holds onboard until the end of the cruise, but food waste, graywater, and blackwater that continue to foul the waters around a number of Caribbean islands frequented by cruise ships.

Increased Enforcement against Dumping

Some Caribbean ports have attempted to tighten enforcement against ocean pollution. The Cayman Islands was perhaps the first to take on the cruise industry when in 1992 it levied a $3,750 fine against the *Seaward* for dumping untreated sewage.[66] A year later it fined Royal Caribbean Cruise Line's *Majesty of the Seas* $2,500 for dumping kitchen waste with an unacceptably high level of bacteria harmful to marine life, and began investigating a second incident involving the *Seaward*.[67] Bermuda also enforced environmental regulations, fining Royal Caribbean's *Nordic Prince* $8,500 in 1992 after deeming it responsible for an oil spill that extended for more than a quarter mile in St. George's harbor.

Other islands are less vigilant. According to David Smith, executive director of Jamaica's Conservation and Development Trust, some Caribbean countries deliberately ignore the law because the governments fear that the cruise line will withdraw their ships if environmental regulations are enforced.[68]

THE PROBLEM OF PEOPLE POLLUTION

Most of us might not consider crowds of people to be an environmental issue, but you need only be in a port when several cruise ships are docked to think otherwise.[69] There are often too many cruise passengers in one place at one time. These huge crowds wear on local people, as evidenced in the love-hate relationship many Alaskan ports have with the cruise industry. While there is noise and congestion — on a typical summer day it is difficult to walk along the downtown streets of many Alaskan ports — there is also the economic benefit derived from all those tourists.

Here are two examples of the problem. In December 1998 I arrived at St. Thomas on a cruise ship — 1 of 13 cruise ships in port that particular day. Imagine 25,000 cruise ship passengers all crammed into the main shopping areas: the downtown and Havensight Mall. While that day was unusual — this was the most cruise ship passengers in a single day for several years — it was an example of there being more people than can be comfortably accommodated in one area. Not all local residents were happy.

It is common for Juneau, Alaska, a city of 30,000, to receive as many as 10,000 visitors in a day. Every year, photos in the *Juneau Empire* illustrate the extreme congestion on city sidewalks when four or five cruise ships visit. The problem is that much greater in the smaller communities. Take Skagway, for example, a city at the northern end of the Inside Passage with a population of under 900. At times 10,000 cruise ship passengers visit Skagway in one day. During a visit in early May 1996, someone told me that by midsummer most residents cannot wait to reclaim their town, to regain the peace and quiet and beauty that attracted them there in the first place. The locals look forward to being able to walk unhindered through town. The same sentiment was expressed in Ketchikan and at other ports frequented by cruise ships.

This overcrowding by cruise passengers doesn't wear only on the locals, it also influences the passengers' experience of the port. Visiting a town such as Skagway is quite different done on your own, with no cruise ships in port, compared to a trip taken early in the season when there may be twice as many cruise ship passengers as city residents. And the experience is different again on those days when there are ten times more visitors than residents. The usual pristine beauty and peaceful environment is nowhere to be found. And as the ships leave, in their wake remains the refuse and environmental wear and tear from thousands of people having been crammed into a relatively small space.

The problem of people pollution is not limited only to Alaska or to Caribbean ports. As the cruise industry grows, more and more ports experience the tourism love-hate relationship: economic benefit versus the people invasion and resulting environmental degradation.

IS THE CRUISE INDUSTRY ENVIRONMENTALLY SUSTAINABLE?

You have to wonder whether the cruise industry is environmentally sustainable. Will environmental regulation and protection keep up with the growth of the cruise industry and the environmental challenges it presents? The answer is not simply yes or no. It is clear that the industry has responded to political and economic pressures to clean up its act, but only when absolutely necessary. The question, then, is whether individuals and governments have the will to keep the industry honest and force it to be environmentally responsible. History has taught us that this is not something the cruise industry will do voluntarily.

BELOW THE PASSENGER DECK

WOULD YOU TAKE THIS JOB? Likely not, but every year thousands of workers from nonindustrialized countries do, when they sign on to work aboard a cruise ship. In addition to the working conditions, cruise ship employees are faced with passengers making naive assumptions about their life onboard the ship.

THE VIEW FROM THE PASSENGER'S PERSPECTIVE

When a cruise ship arrives at a port of call, I have often heard a room steward being asked by a passenger at breakfast or leaving the ship what he plans to do ashore during the day. The passenger is probably unaware that the steward has 20 or more rooms to clean and typically works 12 to 16 hours a day. I have similarly heard dining room waiters asked how they spent their day in port. Passengers forget that while they are there to relax and to explore, the cruise ship staff are given limited time ashore. Often there's barely enough time to make a telephone call home and maybe a quick trip to a store to buy necessary personal items, in order to avoid the price gouging in onboard shops. For most service workers, a day in port is spent in the same way as any other afternoon: resting onboard the ship (often in their cabin) and attempting to reduce sleep deprivation.

PASSENGER FOOD VERSUS STAFF FOOD

For passengers, there may be as many as ten choices for dining; the variety of the food provided is one of the attractions to a cruise. For many workers, however, the food served on the cruise ship simply fills the void. I have had room stewards on both a mass-market cruise line and a luxury cruise line gladly accept fruit from a fruit basket in my room, confessing that they have limited to no access to fresh fruit or vegetables.

A room stewardess with Radisson Seven Seas Cruises told me that she had survived primarily on pasta for the five months she had been aboard. The other food provided in the crew mess was either unpalatable to her or consisted of fish prepared for the Filipino workers. She said she didn't like fish and even if she did, the method of preparation was unattractive to her European tastes. It wasn't a complaint as much as a factual statement of her life onboard.

Like many other European workers on ships, she looked forward to an occasional port call where she could go ashore and have a real meal with quality, palatable food. Those indulgences were, however, expensive, rarely available, and often chosen in place of much-needed sleep or rest.

The naivety is not just about work schedules. As passengers are able to consume unlimited amounts and varieties of food, they assume workers are too. Most passengers don't ask, so they don't know. The daily budget for food served to workers is significantly less than for passengers.

The reality of work on a cruise ship is different from what most workers expect. They sign on, excited about the prospect of getting paid to travel the world aboard a modern and beautiful cruise ship. But they are quickly surprised by the long hours of work for relatively low pay, the basic quality of their accommodations, and the degree of insecurity about keeping their job and maintaining their income. Life below the passenger decks has little resemblance to the life above.

WORK CONDITIONS

Work conditions aboard cruise ships vary widely. As you would expect, officers receive higher salaries, have shorter periods between paid vacations, are provided better accommodations, and may have access to passenger dining rooms. Workers in the deck and engine department and in the galley and laundry are at the other extreme, with some of the lowest salaries, most basic living conditions, and contracts three to four times longer than officers'. Many of these folks work below deck during the day, so they rarely see daylight. Room stewards, waiters, busboys, and other service staff have higher incomes and greater freedom of movement around the ship (due to their job function), but otherwise their situation is similar to that of workers in the engine and deck departments.

No matter what the role or position, almost all workers on a cruise ship put in long hours, day after day, rarely with a day off. The exceptions are entertainers, the cruise director and his or her staff, and concessionaires (such as croupiers, photographers, and store attendants) who generally have better living conditions and higher incomes than laborers. Their access to dining rooms and freedom of movement varies widely from one cruise line to another, but in all cases is greater than that of service providers and maintenance workers.

 **CREW TIME**

The average length of employment for hotel crew on cruise ships has dropped from 3 years in 1970, to 18 months in 1990, to 9 months in 2000.[1]

The average crew member on a cruise ship works 10 straight months without a vacation or a day off. Some workers go 12 months or longer with no break. According to *Ships, Slaves, and Competition*, a recent report by the International Commission on Shipping (ICONS): "The more menial the task, the longer the term of the contract."[2]

I WON'T SEE MY DAUGHTER FOR A YEAR

"Look at this picture of my daughter," says the woman working at the purser's desk aboard the *Statendam*, a Holland America Line cruise ship. "She is one year old today. I haven't seen her for six months, and won't see her again for another six months." The woman is crying. She's from the Philippines and tells me her one glimmer of hope is that, by doing this work, she'll be able to support her mother and her daughter. She hopes she can save enough to give her daughter opportunities that she never had.

Work contracts vary in length by different classes of employees. Most officers work for four months and then have a two-month vacation. Some cruise lines have reduced the work period to three months to make the job more attractive. Some also permit senior officers to have their partner with them for all or part of their contract.

In contrast, on the majority of cruise lines, anyone who works in the dining room and kitchen, in deck and engine maintenance, or in cleaning passenger cabins, has a contract for 9 or 10 months followed by a 2-month vacation. The standard collective agreement suggested by the International Transport Workers' Federation (ITF) specifies that contracts should be for 9 months, although for "operational convenience" this may be extended to 10 months or reduced to 8 months. Regardless, I have met many employees in the hotel department — that is, waiters and busboys, room stewards, bartenders, and deck workers — who work 12 months straight with no days off.

I Work for 12 Months; He Works for 6

A difference in contract length often relates to the worker's home country, sometimes because of the national union to which the worker belongs. For example, a waiter from Italy or Greece will rarely work more than 6 or 7 months without a vacation. In contrast, workers from many Asian countries, including the Philippines, Indonesia, Malaysia, and China often work 10 or 12 months before a vacation is provided. On some ships, workers with different length contracts work side by side, day after day.

A shift in the nationality of service personnel aboard cruise ships has been one of the most visible changes over the years. In the 1960s and 1970s, cruise lines advertised and took pride in having European staff in service roles. A cruise line's reputation often was based on the nationality of its dining room staff and room stewards. The Greek-owned cruise lines, such as Royal Cruise Line, had

 STAFF

Royal Caribbean International estimated it would need 12,000 new hotel staff in the year 2000 and each year thereafter in order to staff dining rooms and to have enough room stewards.[3]

Greek workers. Italian-owned lines, like Sitmar Cruises, had Italian workers. And Norwegian-owned cruise lines, such as Seabourn Cruises, drew almost entirely from Scandinavian countries. The workers often began in low-level positions and worked their way up. Many hotel managers on cruise ships today started in a ship's galley or as cleaners.

Today workers from nonindustrialized countries in Asia, Latin America, and the Caribbean dominate service positions, and there is less opportunity to advance within the system. Increasingly, hotel department managers have been brought onboard with the bulk of their experience in onshore hotels. This subtle difference has a significant effect. The old-style managers had spent their life on a ship; they knew the struggles and challenges of shipboard living. The new-style managers bring shoreside management principles and expect them to work at sea. In most cases, they don't.

Part of this shift is attributable to the incomes demanded by workers. Because it is cheaper to hire workers from nonindustrialized countries, those who previously worked their way up through the ranks (that is, Western Europeans) are no longer hired for entry-level positions.

Another factor is the length of the employment contract. Workers from industrialized countries are unlikely to accept low pay along with long hours and long contracts with no days off. Cruise lines are unlikely to move to shorter contracts because of the time and expense involved in finding and training more workers. Longer contracts mean fewer workers overall.

Variations by Cruise Line

As well as by nationality, contract length varies from cruise line to cruise line. The main deviation from the norm is among cruise lines in the ultraluxury category — Silversea, Seabourn, and Radisson Seven Seas. Their standard contracts for officers are the same as on other cruise lines, but contracts for service personnel are comparatively shorter. On the ultraluxury cruise lines, dining room waiters and room stewards typically work five or six

 **JOBS**

About 100,000 people had jobs on cruise ships in 2001. Another 120,000 workers will be needed over the next five years.[4]

months and then have a two-month vacation. Also, these workers are paid more generous salaries and do not depend on gratuities for the bulk of their income.

How Many Hours Can a Body Work?

Almost everyone employed on a cruise ship works long hours. Although the ITF's standard contract specifies that workers have at least ten hours off duty within each 24-hour period, this is not always the case. With the minimum required hours of rest, the workweek can hold as many as 98 hours.

Standard ITF-approved contracts stipulate that workers in deck and engine departments be paid for a 40-hour week, plus a guaranteed 103 hours of overtime per month. Contracts for workers in the hotel department often include 160 to 170 hours of overtime per month. The result is a typical workweek of more than 80 hours.

The ten hours of required rest may be broken into no more than two periods, one with at least six consecutive hours off duty and the interval between rest periods not exceeding 14 hours. On a practical level, this means that a person may be required to work 14 hours straight — which means that the person serving you in the dining room or navigating on the bridge may have had a break of only six hours since last finishing a work shift.

A 2001 ITF survey of workers on cruise ships docking at Port Canaveral, Florida, provides some insight into the actual hours worked. Almost one-third of crew members indicated they worked 12 or more consecutive hours without a rest period. One-third reported having no rest period longer than six hours. Thirty-seven percent reported having eight-hour rest periods. Only 25 percent reported having ten hours of uninterrupted rest.

This work pace continues day after day, without a day off, for the duration of the contract. More than 95 percent of workers on cruise ships report working seven days a week, week after week. Several studies document the impact of this pace of work. A

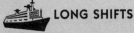 **LONG SHIFTS**

Cruise ship dining room staff and room stewards typically work more than 80 hours a week.

major report by the International Commission on Shipping (ICONS), released in March 2001 under the title *Ships, Slaves, and Competition*, cited the problem of worker fatigue as a major factor in accidents onboard ships.[5] The US Coast Guard independently estimates that fatigue was a factor in 16 percent of critical ship casualties and in 33 percent of personal injury cases.

The debilitating effect of the pace is also quite real. Many workers have told me that their first month of vacation is spent sleeping — they are so worn out from work that it takes that long to catch up and again feel "human." The second month is usually spent with family and friends, but much of the time the employees are preoccupied with the dread of having to return to the ship for another 10- to 12-month period without a day off. So why do they do it? Often the incentive is the knowledge that they are providing for their family. Others hope to save enough money to one day start their own business at home.

Race, Ethnicity, and National Origin

Most cruise ships proudly tell passengers the number of nations represented among the staff, presenting this as a positive feature. But such diversity can undermine collective action by crew. People with dissimilar backgrounds are less likely to cooperatively join forces on an issue. In only a few cases have cruise ship workers attempted collective action.

In 1981 240 Central American workers went on strike aboard a Carnival Cruise Lines ship at Miami to protest the firings of two coworkers. The strike ended quickly when Carnival called US Immigration, declared the strikers illegal immigrants, bused them to the airport, and flew them home.[6]

Similarly, in January 1986 Norwegian Cruise Lines solved a sudden labor dispute aboard the Norway by loading 55 South Korean, Jamaican, and Haitian room stewards onto buses at the Port of Miami and sending them back to their home countries. It's a story I've heard more than once. Paul Chapman paints a similar picture in his book *Trouble on Board: The Plight of International Seafarers*: "On cruise ships, supervisors often tell seafarers who complain, 'If you don't like it here, you can go home.' Since the seafarer has already paid for the return trip, the threat is real and the seafarers know it will be carried out at their expense."[7]

The mediating effects of diversity and the threat that staff will lose their job if they complain are effective mechanisms for keeping workers "in their place" and under control. The workers know to do their jobs without complaining. One worker with Carnival Cruise Line had his pay reduced by $80 after five years with the company. Although clearly upset and unsure what had prompted the reduction, he dared not complain: he feared his supervisors would brand him a troublemaker if he did. He said he would rather endure the pay reduction than lose his job.[8]

Subtle forms of control are exercised in other ways. Holland America Line prides itself on having Indonesian room stewards and dining room waiters. On a cruise aboard the *Veendam*, I asked a busboy who was handing out trays at the Lido buffet (a cafeteria-style dining room) what it was like working with a surveillance camera trained on him — there is a camera in the ceiling, like those in casinos, monitoring activity in the Lido. His response was dispassionate and simple: "The Dutchman is always watching." It became clear that the traditional colonial relationship between the Dutch and Indonesians was replicated on these ships. The Indonesian staff was naturally reverent and deferential to the Dutch bosses, not just as their employer but also as the colonial power under which previous generations grew up.

Diversity on ships can also make workers' lives more difficult. Occasionally fights break out between workers, and there have been stabbings. Likely the most extreme occurrence was a riot in the spring of 1994 when a crew galley ran out of rice. The cook and six others were killed in the riot. This level of violence is uncommon, but tensions between individuals and/or groups are not.

A number of years ago, I heard that an executive chef on Norwegian Cruise Line's *Norway*, a man I knew from several cruises with different cruise lines, had been fired. He was setting up a midnight Chocoholic buffet when a Filipino safety officer walked by, jabbed him in the ribs, and stated ethnic slurs. This pattern was not new; the chef had endured it for weeks. On this occasion, however, he had had enough. He walked into the galley, returned with a fire extinguisher, and emptied the contents onto the safety officer. While the chef lost his job -retrospectively, something he was glad about — the safety officer was merely reprimanded.

On a recent cruise aboard an ultraluxury ship, I observed a dynamic in the dining room between the dominant Austrian (and other Germanic) staff and employees who were clearly non-Germanic. One waiter, the only Italian, was treated less respectfully by supervisors than his Austrian subordinates. In addition, he was responsible for the pasta trolley — a station that prepared fresh pasta dishes at lunch — with his Italian heritage visibly exploited. The overall dynamics, many of which were subtle, led my partner to one day say to this waiter after dinner, "World War II has been over for more than 50 years, but its remnants are still alive here today." The difference in social position was even greater for the lone dark-skinned waiter from Turkey.

Some cruise lines are less subtle in their treatment of certain workers. Many years ago on Regency Cruises, I met a Honduran busboy. I asked him how long it would take for him to be promoted to waiter. He responded matter-of-factly that he would never be promoted: his skin was too dark for a waiter. Several years later a wine steward told me he used to work for Crystal Cruises, but one day the Japanese-owned cruise line fired all its Filipino wine stewards. The fired employees, who were told their skin color and nationality didn't project the company's desired image, were replaced with people of European descent.

Female Employees and Sexual Exploitation

On cruise ships, as in many work settings, female employees often deal with sexual harassment and sexual exploitation. And, as in other work settings, the problem is kept relatively quiet, in large part because the victims are in a vulnerable position that inhibits their ability to speak up.

In his book *Trouble on Board: The Plight of International Seafarers*, Paul Chapman shares insightful comments from an interview with a cruise ship bar waitress:

> Nick, the bar manager, turned out to be nothing but a constant source of trouble. On the second night aboard, he approached Barbara about going to bed with him. She tactfully declined his crude advances — Nick kept up his disgusting pursuit of Barbara. We had a rough time. He

was a disgusting creep who just wouldn't leave us alone, and he was our boss.

When I left that ship, I finally had a phone conversation with the owner. He only laughed at me and said I was wasting his time.... I was very lucky that I had the money to get myself out of the rotten situation; but there are many who are not as fortunate. They have to stay and make the best of it because they have families to support.... [T]hat is the weakness which ... [is exploited.][9]

In an article based on her five years at sea, a young woman whose job it was to produce the ship's daily newspaper tells similar stories. She recounts an officer who refused to take no for an answer and who chased a female crew member so relentlessly that she signed off in tears at a remote port in Alaska.[10]

The problem of sexual harassment was given considerable media attention in late 1999 following discovery hearings in which Carnival Cruise Line admitted to receiving 108 complaints of sexual assault (including 22 rapes — 16 rapes of passengers by crew and six rapes in which one crew member assaulted another) in a five-year period; Royal Caribbean indicated it had received 58 complaints over the same period.

The discovery was part of a lawsuit brought against Carnival Cruise Line by a woman who had worked as a nurse for three years. She claimed she had been raped and sodomized in August 1998 by the ship's engineer, allegedly an experienced sexual predator, while working on the *Imagination*. She had immediately reported the incident, and the engineer was promptly fired. However, his firing was not because of the rape, but because he had been drinking within six hours of going on duty and for being tardy. The case was settled 15 months later, less than two weeks before its scheduled trial.[11]

One year earlier a 54-year-old woman who worked at the gift shop on the *Crystal Harmony* initiated a lawsuit against Crystal Cruises, claiming that the company allowed a sexually charged atmosphere and that she had been fired for refusing the captain's advances. She said that from the start, parties and love affairs were common among crew members.

But more disturbing, she said, was how the ship's top brass hit on stewardesses and other lower-ranking crewmembers.... One ship stewardess confided ... that she was "stressed" over sleeping with 31 crewmembers. And she heard that an officer tried to hang himself after finding his girlfriend in bed with the ship's doctor.... She also said she once encountered the captain and a stewardess in a sex act below deck.[12]

The woman claims she was forced to engage in sex with the captain, for fear that if she refused she would lose her job. She characterized the cruise ship as a more blatant sexually promiscuous environment than any she had ever seen, and said that "the officers and captain think they can take liberty with anyone.... It's quite amazing.... Nobody wants to complain, because they would lose their job."[13]

Is the problem worse on cruise ships than in other work settings? There is no way of knowing because very few complaints become public knowledge. Victims are often not in a position to do anything to correct the situation. As pointed out in the ICONS report, *Ships, Slaves, and Competition*, "crew members who suffer ... sexual assault ... are quickly removed from the ship, usually with no compensation, and access to US courts."[14] This, unfortunately, is part of the reality these women endure to earn a living.

It Isn't Just Female Employees

It is even more difficult to get a clear picture of sexual exploitation of male employees. Given the double stigma of homophobia and the perceived loss of masculinity, male victims rarely report abuses. However, the ITF recently documented several sexual predators working in supervisory positions on cruise ships. Two of them have a 15-year history.

Like the harassment and abuse of women, the victimization of men involves a person in authority using the employee's continued employment and/or opportunity for advancement as a means for extracting sexual favors. The blatancy of the perpetrators' behavior is hard to assess because most victims are unwilling to openly discuss their experiences. At this point, all we know for sure is that such abuse takes place and that it may occur as frequently as the harassment and abuse of women.

$500 for an Interview, $1,000 for the Job

Many laborers and service workers on cruise ships have secured their job through a recruiting agent. Although International Labor Organization (ILO) regulations prohibit agents from collecting fees from the worker — they are supposed to be collected from the employer — workers are often required to pay to secure a position.[15] These payments range from $500 to as much as $4,000.[16]

Paul Chapman's study of international seafarers, *Trouble on Board*, provides insight into the role of the recruiting agent:

> In many cases, seafarers view their recruiting agent, not the captain or the ship owner, as their employer. The agent becomes the seafarer's patron, someone to whom they remain loyal despite abuses. The others in authority are strangers; seafarers often do not know the ship owner, and the officers who give day-to-day orders are often from another country and speak another language. It is the agent with whom the seafarers negotiate the terms of their contract, in whose office employment agreements are signed, and the person who forwards allotment payments to their families.[17]

The cost to the employee is not trivial. A 1997 story in the *Wall Street Journal* cites a Croatian worker who paid $600 to an agent to confirm his employment.[18] In addition, he started work with a $1,400 debt to Carnival Cruise Line, which had advanced the cost of his transportation to the ship.

In February 2000 an article in the *Miami New Times* described a cook on Carnival Cruise Line's *Paradise* who had given a Bombay agency $2,000, an amount which included airfare.[19] That sum, much of which he had borrowed from relatives, is almost one-third of the $7,000 he would make during his ten-month contract.

In 2001 I was told of an agent in Romania charging $500 to interview for a position with Norwegian Cruise Line. If a person was hired, he or she would be required to pay an additional

$1,000 to secure the position. It would take the worker at least two months to recoup this expense.

An obvious question is, why do workers tolerate such situations? Because, simply put, they need the job and they naively believe that the cruise ship will provide career opportunities. Once onboard, they tolerate continued abuses because they know that to speak up would mean losing their job. It isn't just a matter that they would be sent home, but in many cases they have not yet earned enough to cover the expenses incurred in securing the employment, including return airfare.[20]

Contrary to ITF-approved standard contracts that require travel expenses to be borne by the employer, it is not uncommon for workers to have to pay for their own transportation and, upon arrival at the ship, to have to deposit an open ticket for their return flight home. Upon dismissal, the cruise line simply makes flight arrangements for that ticket.

The harsh reality of going into debt to secure employment is further reflected in how workers deal with job loss. I became aware of this issue when my partner and I were on a cruise in 1994. While we were sitting on the deck waiting to disembark, we were joined by the food and beverage manager, a man we knew through two previous cruises. We asked him how he was. He responded that he had been up all night and proceeded to tell us that he was firing 33 workers. He had spent the night making arrangements for their flights home and was now preparing to let them know that they were headed home that afternoon. He explained that he waited until the last minute to prevent harm to the ship and to prevent the workers from harming themselves.

This last comment appeared self-serving until several years later. In August 1998 I read a newspaper account of the death of a 28-year-old Turkish woman. Upon learning she was going to be fired from her job aboard Holland America Line's *Westerdam*, she committed suicide by jumping overboard as the ship approached Vancouver harbor.

In many cases, between the debt incurred to get the job and the humiliation of having to return home after being fired, workers see few alternatives. It is hard to know how common suicides are among ship's crew because this is not regularly reported in the mass media, but more than once, unfortunately, cruise ship workers have told me about employee suicides, and on one occasion I was onboard a ship when one of its employees took his own life.

INCOMES

Like the length of contracts, the wages paid by cruise lines also vary widely. In the ultraluxury category, a waiter working for Seabourn Cruises earns approximately $3,000 a month before tips; in contrast, a waitress with Radisson Seven Seas Cruises earns $2,000 a month before tips. Waiters' wages on the premium cruise lines also vary. Holland America Line, which has a policy of "tipping not required," pays its waiters $300 a month. Celebrity Cruises pays its waiters a mere $50 a month and then charges $7 a week for breakage — whether or not anything has been broken. Mass-market cruise lines pay salaries similar to those of Celebrity Cruises. On most cruise ships, service personnel earn the bulk of their income from gratuities; Silversea, Seabourn and Radisson are exceptions.

 **CENTS PER HOUR**

A janitor who has been employed by Carnival Cruise Line for five years works 70 hours a week and earns $372 a month — a wage that works out to less than $1.55 an hour.[22]

It is difficult to get reliable figures regarding pay rates. No cruise line releases this information. Much of what I know has been gleaned from workers, from investigative journalists, from investigations done by labor groups, and from testimony presented in congressional hearings.[21]

See Table 5.1 for an indication of the salaries (including vacation pay) specified in a typical ITF-approved contract for a ship operating solely in Europe and serving a largely Western European clientele. The contract wage is guaranteed in case of illness or where tips are insufficient.

Table 5.1

SAMPLE PAY SCALE ON A CRUISE SHIP, 2000-01
(US$ PER MONTH)

Deck and Engine Department

Position*	Base Pay	Guaranteed Overtime†	Weekend Overtime	Leave	Monthly Total
Master	1,916	969	498	662	4,045
Chief engineer	1,748	884	454	615	3,701
Staff captain	1,142	578	297	446	2,462
1st officer	998	505	259	405	2,167
2nd officer	915	463	238	382	1,998
3rd officer	882	446	229	372	1,929
1st electrician	786	398	205	346	1,735
Bosun	587	297	152	290	1,326
Able seafarer	525	266	136	273	1,200
Security guard	525	266	136	273	1,200
O.S./wiper‡	381	192	99	233	905
Utility	314	159	82	214	769
Trainee	289	146	75	207	717

Hotel Department

Position*	Base Pay	Guaranteed Overtime†	Weekend Overtime	Leave	Monthly Total
Hotel manager	1,461	1,007	747	175	3,390
Cruise director	1,368	942	700	164	3,174
F&B manager‡	1,368	942	700	164	3,174
Chief purser	974	671	498	117	2,260
Chief steward	761	524	389	91	1,765
Excursion manager	730	503	373	88	1,694
Maitre d'hotel	704	485	360	85	1,634
Head waiter	483	433	247	57	1,120
Waiter/steward	435	300	222	52	1,009§
Busboy	317	219	162	38	736§
Cleaner	261	102	133	31	527
Trainee	239	93	122	29	483

Kitchen					
Position*	Base Pay	Guaranteed Overtime†	Weekend Overtime	Leave	Monthly Total
Executive chef	1,368	942	700	164	3,174
Sous chef	483	333	247	58	1,121
1st baker	296	204	151	35	686
2nd cook	278	192	142	33	645
3rd cook	270	185	138	32	625
Cleaner	261	102	133	31	527
Trainee	239	993	122	29	483

General					
Position*	Base Pay	Guaranteed Overtime†	Weekend Overtime	Leave	Monthly Total
Doctor	1,523	1049	779	183	3,534
Nurse	543	374	278	65	1,260
Hairdresser	435	300	222	52	1,009
Laundry master	435	300	222	52	1,009
Tailor	283	194	145	34	656
Garbage/utility	261	102	133	31	527

Source: International Transport Workers' Federation. By agreement, I have not
identified the ship.

* Most of the above listed positions are for contracted employees; some are
concessionaires.

† In the deck and engine department, the guaranteed total overtime is 103
hours per month; in other departments, it is 162 hours per month.

‡ O.S. = ordinary seaman; F&B = food and beverage.

§This is the guaranteed wage including tips.

Some officers, particularly those who head a department and
manage its budget, are able to augment their salaries with year-end
bonuses.[23] Many companies pay a percentage bonus to the master,
chief engineer, and hotel manager for staying under budget. In
some cases bonuses are shared with others in the officer's department. Others, such as doctors[24] and salespeople, receive commis-
sions based on generated income.

No Minimum Wage

In reviewing the salary figures shown in Table 5.1 it is necessary to keep three things in mind. First, these rates of pay are for workers covered under ITF-approved contracts. Not all cruise lines have contracts consistent with these standards. Carnival Cruise Line and Disney Cruise Line are the only large North American carriers without such an agreement.

Second, workers who receive tips have their income from gratuities included in their guaranteed monthly income. Consequently, on most mass-market and some premium cruise lines, waiters and room stewards earn base salaries of $50 per month. The remainder of their income is drawn from tips. The cruise line guarantees a certain salary level in case tips are insufficient to reach the minimum salary provided by contract.

Third, there is no minimum wage law covering cruise ships. Because most cruise ships are registered in countries other than the USA — using what are called "flags of convenience" — it is the labor laws of those countries that apply to work conditions and to wages. Congress has attempted to bring ships operating out of American ports under American labor laws, but so far unsuccessfully.

The closest that Congress came to imposing American law on foreign-flagged cruise ships operating from American ports was in 1993. In the course of congressional hearings, the International Council of Cruise Lines (ICCL) threatened that the cruise industry would leave American ports (and relocate to non-American ports) if Congress passed the proposed legislation. ICCL president John Estes pointed out how easily cruise ships could be moved from one homeport to another, and that

> in order to keep international costs competitive we do in fact on occasion move from country to country. International shipping will always seek a hospitable economic and political climate from which to operate ... It would be an unfortunate failure of United States policy not to recognize that homeports are unimportant to passengers.[25]

WHEN DOES $10 EQUAL $1,000,000?

A number of years ago, I was on a cruise aboard Holland America Line's *Rotterdam*. Every morning at 7:00, a Filipino deck boy would set up lounge chairs and cushions on the back decks. Midmorning and mid-afternoon he served beverages; every evening he collected dirty towels, restacked the chairs and cushions, and cleared out the garbage recepta-cles. This was his routine every day of the week for the full duration of his 14-month contract, without a day off.

I noticed that every morning he would set up two chairs at the back of the pool deck. They faced out to the sea, had extra towels, and by 7:30 every morning would have the passengers' belongings there to reserve them for the day. On the fourth day I asked the young man about the chairs. He said, "Oh, those are for Mr. Larry. When he comes on the ship he expects me to do this for him." It became apparent that the expectation was not rewarded with any kind words nor any form of gratuity. On the last day of the cruise, as a gesture for the kindness he had shown me, I handed the deck boy a folded $10 bill. He flatly refused to take it. When I slipped it into his shirt pocket, tears came to his eyes and he expressed the warmest appreciation I have ever felt.

While to me the $10 was throwaway money, to him it was quite a bit more. I learned later the value of what I gave him; his monthly income was roughly $250. The knowledge that such a small gesture could mean so much was worth considerably more than what it cost.

Ultimately, the 1993 effort was unsuccessful. Hopes for future congressional intervention ended in 1995 with election of a Republican majority. Without congressional intervention, workers with cruise lines that abide by ITF guidelines earn incomes that, by American and Canadian standards, are dreadfully low for the number of hours worked. Those people working for cruise lines that either ignore or circumvent ITF guidelines are left with the choice of either accepting the situation or being unemployed. Neither choice is particularly attractive.

But Look at the Tips Received by Service Personnel

Despite all that, many passengers think that room stewards, dining room waiters, and busboys are making scads of money. Why? Because of the cruise line's recommendations for minimum tips. The industry norm per passenger is $3.50 a day for waiters, $2.00 a day for busboys, and $3.50 a day for room stewards. Some cruise lines also recommend passengers pay a tip of $1.00 a day to dining room headwaiters and/or the maitre d'.

If waiters were able to keep all of that money, their income might be reasonable. However, workers may be expected, if not required, to share their tips with others. Some maitre d's expect waiters to hand over six to ten percent of their tips; chief stewards expect the same from room stewards. There isn't much a worker can do. In the case of a dining room waiter, the maitre d' decides which station (area of the ship) the waiter will work in — a station with big tippers or another where income is low. In addition, the amount of shared tips may influence the number of passengers the waiter is responsible for serving and the location of his or her station. The more waiters pay, the better their situation.

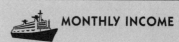 **MONTHLY INCOME**

In the year 2000 more than half of cruise ship workers reported a monthly income of less than $1,000. Among respondents to an ITF-administered survey of workers on ships homeported at Port Canaveral, Florida, 16 percent earned less than $500 per month, 38 percent earned between $500 and $999, 19 percent earned between $1,000 and $1,499, 17 percent between $1,500 and $2,000, and 12 percent earned over $2,000. (Percentages do not add up to 100 due to rounding off of figures.)

Cruise ship hotel workers often have to make under-the-table payments to staff with the power to affect their situation. For example, a room steward may pay people in the laundry in order to be among the first to receive clean linens. A dining room waiter might pay workers in the galley to ensure that food orders are warm. This onboard mafia is kept quiet and is only scarcely discussed.[27] I first learned of it from a ship's physician. The physician hears about it because she or he is an independent concessionaire, unbeholden to the company, and seen by workers as their personal doctor, obligated to maintain strict confidentiality.

For Your Convenience, We Now Centralize Payment of Tips

In recent years several cruise lines have begun centralizing payment of gratuities. Norwegian Cruise Line and Princess Cruises automatically charge $10 a day to passengers' onboard accounts. Other cruise lines have experimented with the system on certain of their ships. Passengers are told this is done for their convenience. However, the real agenda is that, as the number of alternative restaurants onboard a ship increases — resulting in passengers no longer having the same waiter for the duration of the cruise — the cruise lines want to ensure that tips cover all of workers' salaries. Without a centralized payment system, the company would have to make up any difference between tips individually received and the minimum income level provided under the ITF-approved contract.

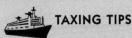 **TAXING TIPS**

According to the ITF, cruise ship maitre d's have been reported to earn as much as $14,000 to $20,000 a month — more than $200,000 per year — from taxing workers' tips.[26]

Although it is difficult to know for certain, it appears that centralization of tips is a means to deal with the onboard mafia — the system of taxing tips and of workers feeling pressured to pay off whoever has the ability to affect their job. Headwaiters and maitre d's now presumably receive an amount from the company based on total tips received. Waiters, busboys, and room stewards also receive their tips from the company. It is unclear how the tips collected are distributed and whether workers actually receive the full amount that the cruise line recommends passengers pay. While covert abuses may be reduced, the company may now simply have institutionalized the system of payoffs.

In the end, many workers likely earn less now than they did under the old system where tips were paid directly to them for the services they provided.

THE ART OF WORKING FOR TIPS

Some cruise lines do still encourage the payment of gratuities directly to workers. A job in the hotel department, as a waiter, busboy, or room steward, on these cruise lines means that your income depends largely on generating tips.

A certain attitude must be maintained: a worker must assume the role of a humble servant, yet at the same time also be comfortable talking about his or her home and family. The latter can be particularly stressful, given the fact that workers commonly miss their family and loved ones. Talking about them can be difficult, particularly when it may be as long as eight or nine months until they see them again (or since they saw them). Add to this the fact that workers serve as many as 40 new passengers every week, and a substantial number of those passengers converse about the same thing, week after week. The stress of these conversations must be kept in check because cordiality and responsiveness are important elements in the size of tips a worker receives.

Workers must also be tolerant of passengers who like to talk about themselves, their family, or their economic successes. Cruise passengers forget, or don't care, that cruise ship workers are often from nonindustrialized countries

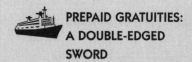

PREPAID GRATUITIES: A DOUBLE-EDGED SWORD

In the past, most frontline workers — waiters, stewards, and busboys — on cruise ships had greatest fear for their future from onboard managers, who could fire them without reason and also influence their income from salary and/or tips. With prepaid tips, they also live in constant fear that passengers could cause them to lose their jobs. On some cruise lines, some passengers pay tips in advance by credit card but then cancel the charges at the end of the cruise. There's not a thing an employee can do about this, and it means that he or she is subject to an automatic review by the company. In other words, employees may lose both their money and their job.

With the current practice of gratuities being applied to onboard accounts, there may be similar reviews and sanctions. While charging gratuities on onboard accounts is presented as being done for the convenience of passengers, there may be other goals being served. No matter, in the end it is the worker who is likely to suffer.[28]

where many of the things passengers take for granted are either unavailable or too expensive. Passengers tend to ignore the fact that the economic and social system in the worker's homeland may be very different from their own.

The issue may be as fundamental as religion. On Holland America Line, for example, passengers traveling in December often wish workers a Merry Christmas. They assume that the workers celebrate the holiday; if the workers don't, they are unlikely to correct the passenger. The fact is, on this particular cruise line, the majority of the Indonesian staff is Muslim. One year I conveyed good wishes to my waiter for his celebration of Ramadan. He was initially surprised that a passenger knew about the Muslim holy month. My statement of awareness of his culture and beliefs changed the manner in which he treated my partner and me through the remainder of the cruise. But at the same time, he continued to play the role for other passengers who assumed he was Christian. He even tolerated comments about how cute he was. Workers learn to keep many parts of themselves private and to discuss what they know from experience passengers want to hear. Much of who they really are remains hidden.

Through experience, workers learn and adopt tricks to ingratiate themselves to the people they serve. On many cruise lines, room stewards lay out passengers' pajamas or towels in the shape of animals when they turn down the beds for the night. Many passengers like this. Often it is even expected — not infrequently, individuals post messages on Internet discussion groups expressing disappointment that their steward did not do this, or they didn't do it as well as others had led them to expect.

Dining room waiters have learned to compliment passengers on their meal choices. Some passengers take these as positive statements about themselves as a person and view their waiter more positively. Waiters might bring an extra dessert or a dessert with a scoop of ice cream. They have learned that these gestures produce positive reactions and presumably result in larger tips.

ITF CAMPAIGNS AND CRUISE SHIP WORKERS

Closely allied with its efforts to raise pay standards on cruise ships is the International Transport Workers' Federation (ITF) campaign against flags of convenience.[29] In the past, when ships were owned and registered in the same country, they were crewed mostly by people from that country. Workers could turn to their national trade unions, not only for the establishment and assurance of decent working conditions and wages, but also in the event of difficulties.

On international vessels using a flag of convenience, however, seafarers no longer have this ability. Onboard regulation is arbitrarily set by company policy; the main goal is profit. Workers in the deck and engine department, with no opportunity for tips, live with low wages and less-than-optimal living conditions.

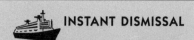 **INSTANT DISMISSAL**

The 2000 ICONS report *Ships, Slaves, and Competition* reveals that the "contracts [of some cruise ship workers] include a clause that provides for instant dismissal if any contact is made with an ITF representative…. Crew members dismissed for complaining about work conditions, or for speaking to ITF officials, find themselves blacklisted by manning agents when they return home. This means that they will likely never be rehired on any ship."[30]

Sailing under a flag of convenience is common practice in the shipping industry generally, not just within the cruise industry. The practice presents problems for workers, but economic incentives for ship owners and operators.

What Is a Flag of Convenience?

A "flag of convenience" ship is one that flies the flag of a country other than the country of ownership. For example, the major cruise lines serving North America are headquartered in the United States and owned by American interests; the two largest conglomerates have their stocks trade on the New York Stock Exchange.

Although the beneficial ownership of these companies is in the United States, the flags flown on all of their vessels are those of other countries. The most common flags are of the Bahamas, Liberia, and Panama. In 1999 approximately 62 percent of cruise ships were registered in these countries, pretty much evenly divided between the three. Of this group, Panama is considered the most deficient flag state — in terms of safety and exploitation of seafarers — in the world.[32]

 **PROFIT**

In 1999 and again in 2000, Carnival Corporation earned profits of approximately $1 billion — and paid virtually no corporate income tax.[31]

A number of ships left Liberian registry in 2001 following disclosure that fees collected were being used to fund the Revolutionary United Front in Sierra Leone and for armed militias in Liberia. Most of these ships transferred to either Panama or the Bahamas.

In recent years other ships have been registered in the United Kingdom, the Netherlands, France, and Italy. These countries do not provide flags of convenience, but have in almost all cases provided financial incentives for these registrations — in some cases, providing substantial shipbuilding subsidies in return for the registration. Although the ships registered in these countries may be owned elsewhere, the cruise line involved has an identity with the country of registration; for example, Cunard Line and the United Kingdom; Holland America Line and the Netherlands; Costa Cruises and Italy.

At the same time, other ships have shifted to flags of convenience. Seabourn Cruises moved from Norway to the Bahamas in 2002; Silversea Cruises shifted two of its ships from Italy to the Bahamas; and several years ago Radisson Seven Seas Cruises changed ships previously registered in Finland and Norway to the Bahamas. In early 2002 there were rumors that Royal Olympic Cruises, which has traditionally used the Greek flag, was considering registering its newest ship in Malta.

What attracts cruise lines to flags of convenience? Money: cheap registration fees, low or no taxes, freedom to employ cheap labor. As foreign corporations, they avoid virtually all US taxes. Royal Caribbean Cruises Limited pays no corporate income tax, and Carnival Corporation pays tax only on its land-based operations in Alaska through Holland America/Westours. As well, because the cruise lines are subject to the laws of the country in which they are registered, their ships operate free of American labor laws and many other regulations. During the proposed merger of Princess Cruises and Royal Caribbean Cruises Limited, a key issue was whether the arrangement would preserve each

Table 5.2

FLAGS USED BY MAJOR CRUISE LINES, 2002

Cruise Line	Country of Registration
Carnival Cruise Line	Liberia, Panama
Celebrity Cruises	Liberia, Panama
Crystal Cruises	Bahamas
Cunard Line	Britain
Disney Cruise Line	Bahamas
Holland America Line	Bahamas, Netherlands
Norwegian Cruise Line	Bahamas
Orient Line	Bahamas
Princess Cruises	Bahamas, Bermuda, Britain, Italy, Liberia
Radisson Seven Seas	Bahamas, France
Royal Caribbean International	Liberia, Norway
Seabourn Cruise Line	Bahamas
Silversea Cruises	Bahamas
Windstar Cruises	Bahamas

company's tax-free status. Provided documents assured stock-holders of both companies that there would be no individual or corporate tax liability. Lawyers for Carnival Corporation — a competitor in the proposed merger with P&O Princess — expressed a different opinion.

The goal of the ITF campaign against flags of convenience — to shift the registry of ships to the country in which there is beneficial ownership of both the ship and the cruise line — is consistent with provisions of the United Nations Law of the Sea. Workers would benefit in that they are likely to have greater protection and rights under the laws of the United States or countries such as Norway, Italy, or the United Kingdom where many cruise lines are based and owned. The argument against these

A FEW WORDS ON FLAGS OF CONVENIENCE

A flag of convenience provides a low-cost option for ship registry. It also allows a company to operate a ship with fewer regulations or controls than would be the case if it was registered in the United States. Worker salaries and hours are not regulated by American labor laws, and workers have limited if any recourse in American or other courts if there is a dispute over wages or a workplace injury. For example, one cruise ship company's contract states:

> The Employee shall be initially employed on board the ship stated in the Employment Agreement and shall be subject to the rights and obligations as are set forth in the Maritime Laws of the Bahamas. Employer and Employee agree that any dispute or claims arising under this Agreement shall be governed and adjudicated pursuant to laws of the Bahamas, regardless of any other legal remedies that may be available.[33]

Foreign registries also leave the inspection and certification of safety equipment to the US Coast Guard (or similar authority in some European countries). Ships that don't stop at American ports may never be fully inspected.

The flag of convenience is an economic benefit to the cruise line and easy to purchase. Liberia offers its registry through International Registries in Reston, Virginia. Panama's fleet-safety and registration operation is based in Manhattan, not in Panama City.

Ship registry has become big business. In 1995 Panama earned $47.5 million in ship registration fees and annual taxes — 5 percent of its federal budget — and another $50 million in fees for maritime lawyers, agents, and inspectors. The Panamanian government operates 56 maritime consulates around the world from which a registration can be purchased. The consul receives a cash bonus based on the amount of business brought in, and for transfer of multiple ships to Panamanian registry, can offer discounts of up to 50 percent as well as, in some cases, a complete waiver of fees for a year.[34]

changes, generally advanced by the cruise lines, is that operating costs would increase and, ultimately, so would the price of a cruise.

The ITF and Female Workers

The ITF is also engaged in a campaign to protect the rights of female workers — efforts that go well beyond only female employees on cruise ships. In 1999 the ITF Women's Committee extended its campaign to women's basic rights, to make it more inclusive. In addition to issues such as equal access and freedom from discrimination, the committee has worked for women's freedom from sexual harassment and violence. This includes not just providing a place to turn in cases where a female employee has been harassed or exploited, but also clear guidelines for collective agreements that will protect women from the fear of harassment and violence. As well, the ITF provides female workers with tips for survival — a sort of self-defense guide.

The ITF's Seafarers' Section — the division concerned with workers on ships — has also taken a role in protecting workers. It has developed policy guidelines on harassment and bullying. Rooted in the United Nations Universal Declaration of Human Rights, the guidelines are designed for both employers and employees. As in any other workplace, workers aboard ships may be hesitant — or on a practical level, unable — to exercise their rights under these guidelines. The cruise industry has a history of not cooperating with the ITF, nor with others interested in the welfare and well-being of people working on cruise ships.

A SWEATSHOP OR NOT?

A cruise ship may not fit neatly into the conventional definition of the term "sweatshop," but regardless, the work conditions and rates of pay are certainly below standards common in the North America, Western Europe, and Australia. The vast majority of cruise ship passengers are drawn from these countries, lured by economical vacation packages, but it is the workers on whose backs their bargain rests. Despite bargain pricing, the cruise line earns a hefty profit.

EVERYTHING WOULD RUN FINE ... BUT PASSENGERS KEEP GETTING IN THE WAY

AFTER COMPLETING A PRE-CRUISE PACKAGE at a hotel in San Juan, Puerto Rico, my partner and I show up, along with five or six other couples, at the assigned time for transportation from the hotel to the ship. After ten minutes or so, someone inquires about the bus and is told, "It will be here soon." Ten minutes later, my partner and I tire of waiting. We jump into a cab and head to the ship, leaving the others behind. Onboard the ship that evening we learn that although those waiting had made several phone calls, it had taken almost two hours for a bus to arrive. Eventually it came out that the reason for the delay was that originally no bus had been hired to pick us up.

After this cruise I wrote to the company about this and several other lapses — for example, that my cruise line-issued air tickets had me leaving from Boston but returning to Philadelphia, that our room on the ship had inadequate air conditioning, and that special arrangements for the dining room, confirmed in Miami, had been ignored. The response I received concluded by stating:

> We value the opinions and observations of our passengers and wish to assure you that the situations cited were exceptions, rather than the norm at Norwegian Cruise Line. For this reason, we invite your continued patronage, so we may demonstrate to you the high standards that have earned us the fine reputation we enjoy in the travel industry.

After having taken seven cruises, which included 73 days on Norwegian Cruise Line ships, my partner and I decided it was time to try a different company. Unfortunately, the nature of the written response from Norwegian Cruise Line is not unique. Similar letters can be found at carnivalsucks.com, ncl-sucks.com, and on websites named "An NCL Cruise Experience" and "NCL Ruined Our Honeymoon." A UK website detailing a passenger's experiences, with accompanying photos, on the millennium cruise aboard Cunard Line's *QE 2* was short-lived. This was one of the few cases where a cruise line has "settled" with a disgruntled passenger to silence a public display.[1]

Most people go on a cruise expecting everything will go smoothly and there will be no problems, and often, this is the case. However, given the number of possible things that can go wrong, it is not uncommon that something does. Cruise lines vary widely in how they deal with problems. As one journalist states, "When cruises go awry, you're at the mercy of line."[2] Often, the attitude exhibited toward passengers is less than consumer friendly.

CRUISE LINES AND CUSTOMER SATISFACTION

The cruise industry is, like most businesses, providing a service. The companies are able to please many of their customers, but a few have a less than acceptable experience.

Two factors affect whether a customer's complaint will be adequately handled. One is the cruise line's tolerance for customer dissatisfaction. The chief executive officer of one company admitted to me that he expects between 5 and 10 percent of passengers to leave a cruise dissatisfied — which means that a 3,000-passenger ship could have as many as 300 disgruntled passengers every week. In this case, passengers who complain will likely receive a "variation on a theme" form letter and maybe a certificate for 10, 15, or 20 percent off a future cruise.

The cruise line's responsiveness is further influenced by a growing desensitization to consumer complaints. With a high volume of passengers and the range of expectations, cruise lines quickly hear it all and understandably become desensitized to complaints. While producing high expectations through advertising and brochures, they become overwhelmed with customer disappointments. I would not be surprised if as many would-be repeat passengers are turned away by the nature of "customer relations" as by their actual experience on a cruise.

DEALING WITH THE USUAL PROBLEMS

A range of problems can be considered normal occurrences on cruise ships. These things happen often enough that the company has worked out commensurate compensation. Most cruise lines have standard responses for late delivery of new ships, for mechanical problems or mechanical failures, for foodborne or other ship-wide illness, and for overbooking. Minor occurrences such as an

---

 IS THERE LOGIC IN OFFERS OF COMPENSATION?

After Festival Cruises' *Mistral* went aground for 36 hours in the Caribbean in February 2001, the cruise line offered passengers a refund equal to two days' fare. Although provided with free drinks from the ship's bars during the ordeal, many passengers complained of being denied access to telephones. They were out of range for use of cell phones. Many passengers were dissatisfied with the cruise line's offer and planned a coordinated action against the company,[3] although there is no report indicating whether they were successful.

Four months later, the same company provided members of the White House press corps with a certificate for a free cruise, along with a letter from the CEO stating: "Please be assured that your enjoyment is of paramount importance to us all and it gives me great pleasure to offer you a cruise with Festival on any of our new generation ships at any time you choose over the next year as my personal guest."[4] The offer was made to reporters who had been housed on the *Azur* in Genoa harbor during the Group of Eight summit of major industrial democracies, in response to complaints from several reporters about the size and uncleanness of the cabins.

Why such a contrast between the gesture on the *Azur* and the offer given to those on the *Mistral*? The treatment of *Azur* passengers exceeds by far any response I have received when my cabin has been grossly unclean. It suggests that response to problems is, in part, a reflection of the problem, and perhaps in larger part, a reflection of who it was that complained.

injury from a fall or a slight lapse in service are often smoothed over with a the offer of a complimentary bottle of wine or a discount on a future cruise. When I arrived at my penthouse suite on a cruise aboard the *Carnival Destiny*, there was no bedspread on the bed — I was told they didn't have one that fit when the bed was made as a king-size rather than two twins. I complained to the hotel manager, who sent me a certificate for 15 percent off a future cruise — but no bedspread.

The nature of compensation varies widely. Sometimes it makes sense, other times it doesn't. Maybe it depends on how important the cruise line thinks you are. Why else would the same company offer a partial refund to one group of passengers on a grounded cruise ship, and an entire free cruise to another group of passengers who were given unclean cabins?

Upgrades

In recent years cruise lines have produced expectations for upgrades and freebies. Increasingly, passengers book a cruise and expect their accommodations to be upgraded when they arrive on the ship. The expectation comes in part from travel agents who, like passengers, base expectations on past cruise line behavior. They know of cases where a person has been upgraded. Expectations are reinforced by stories told on Internet discussion groups or among friends. In most cases, there is no ready explanation for an upgrade.

An upgrade may be given for a number of reasons. Someone else might request the cabin you reserved; to accommodate that request, you are upgraded to another cabin without reason to ask why. An upgrade may be given to a repeat passenger as a gesture of goodwill, to a new passenger in order to breed loyalty, or to compensate a past passenger for a problem or disappointment on a previous cruise.

No matter the reason for an upgrade, the effect is an increasing awareness that upgrades are given. Many passengers have come to expect upgrades and are disappointed when one is not provided.

Freebies

Cruise lines have also undermined customer satisfaction by giving freebies. At one extreme are compensation packages given when cruises have been canceled or accidents have occurred at sea. In these situations passengers are often offered a refund and a free cruise for their inconvenience. Although appropriate in certain circumstances, this practice does produce awareness that sometimes free cruises are given. Passengers with less serious problems don't always distinguish between their disappointment and these more serious situations; they expect that they, too, deserve a free cruise.

A traditional response to problems aboard cruise ships is to send a complimentary bottle of wine to a passenger's cabin or dinner table. It is uncanny how predictable this is. In June 2001 I appeared on a syndicated call-in radio talk show. One caller began telling a story about an accident involving a slip and fall on a cruise ship. Her husband required stitches but was not seriously injured. As the woman was about to finish her story, I said, "Let me guess. A bottle of wine was sent to your table that night." She responded, "How did you know? One was sent with a signed card from the hotel manager."

 PLEASE ACCEPT OUR APOLOGIES AND THIS BOTTLE OF WINE

The practice of giving a bottle of wine to ameliorate a problem has become so common that some passengers complain purely with the intent of getting that free bottle of wine.

- There is a problem with your plumbing? Have a bottle of wine on us.
- Your room isn't properly cleaned? Accept this gift of a bottle of wine.
- You found something in your food? Here's a bottle of wine.

Indeed, the response has become so routine that some passengers have begun to scam the cruise line. An executive chef with Norwegian Cruise Lines indicated that almost once a week a passenger puts something in his or her food, calls the maitre d' over, and asks for compensation. Even though the object in the food is clearly not something that could have originated in the galley, the passenger receives a free bottle of wine and is pleased with his or her efforts.

Cruise lines are sincere in their gestures, but they are also aware of this cult of expectation. In some ways, they play into it — it's easy to provide something of minimal cost that keeps people happy in the process. The negative side, however, is the growing skepticism about complaints. Very often, crew members view all passenger complaints as attempts to get something for free. The result is that justified complaints can be overlooked or dismissed.

I have many times had a concern dismissed with a response along the lines of "Other passengers haven't mentioned that." The statement invalidates my concern and makes me feel as though the problem is me, not the situation in question. The lesson quickly learned is that if you need to complain, be sure it is about something "normal." Be prepared to have your complaint dismissed if it is anything that has not been heard before, or

 PROBLEMS WITH AIR CONDITIONING

On five separate cruises I have experienced problems with air conditioning. In one case, there was no air conditioning at all; in the other cases, the air conditioning was inadequate. In each case, when the matter was brought to the attention of the purser's desk, the response was that staff were unaware of any problem with the air conditioning. They simply denied that the problem existed.

- Regency Cruises' *Regent Sea* was on its fourth cruise in a row without air conditioning. Staff had been sleeping on the outside decks for the past couple of weeks because of the heat in their cabins, but they were instructed to say that there was no problem. Four days into the cruise, after assurances that repairs were under way, passengers were notified that there was no air conditioning.

- Norwegian Cruise Line's *Norwegian Sea* had its air conditioning turned off for maintenance. Despite dozens of complaints, the purser's desk insisted that there were no problems. Passengers were told that the problem must be isolated to their own cabin and that a technician would be down to make repairs. After seven or eight hours, the system was turned back on.

ignored if it is something like air conditioning over which the person you are talking to has absolutely no control, and no better idea than you if something is wrong or whether it will be fixed.

DEALING WITH THE UNUSUAL

Dealing with an unusual problem can be even more frustrating. A cabin that is not properly cleaned, a service provider who falls short of performance expectations, or a room with malfunctioning air conditioning can each become difficult to deal with. Your complaint will be taken and an effort made to fix the problem, but there is no guarantee that the situation will change. Repeated attempts to have something corrected are often fruitless. Complaining to the cruise line after you get home often only increases your frustration.

- Holland America Line's *Rotterdam* was well known for having problems with its air conditioning during the ship's first year of operation. On a cruise shortly after its first-year anniversary, I had a cabin that never got cool enough for a comfortable night's sleep. After five attempts to have the problem repaired, I discussed the situation with the passenger relations manager. She responded that the ship had never had any problems with the air conditioning. Rather than argue the point, I moved along. As I walked by the purser's desk, I overheard a passenger from a suite, who had the same complaint, being told, "Yes, there's a problem." The proposed solution? The passenger was told to prop a trashcan in the doorway to the veranda as a means of improving air circulation.

- While occupying a suite aboard Holland America Line's *Statendam*, I experienced problems with the air conditioning. Because it was denied that the problem existed, it took four calls, and almost six hours, before a repair-person was sent. The cause turned out to be a faulty thermostat. The air-conditioning engineer volunteered that there was a design problem with all Statendam-class ships and that the air conditioning is a habitual problem on each of them.

Once, I arrived onboard Norwegian Cruise Line's *Windward* only to find my veranda cabin was unclean: there was a broken wine glass on the carpet, mildew stains on the shower curtain, and splatters of some sort of liquid on the walls. After I complained, most of the glass was swept up and the shower curtain was replaced with one that was clean but badly frayed and unsightly; the walls were left as they were. Because the room steward had been forced to "fix" the deficiencies, his service during the cruise included a heavy dose of attitude. We ended up suffering for our expectation of a clean cabin.

In the case of the *Windward*, at least an effort was made to rectify the situation. However, I could cite other situations in which problems were not addressed at all.

There are two reasons why a problem is likely to be ignored. First, the ship is a small community where the staff lives; the members have to get along with one another. There are implications for supervisors when they criticize or must discipline a worker. Doing so may affect the supervisor's reputation, his or her relationship with others in the small community, and could disrupt arrangements where the workers share a portion of their tips. It is easier to ignore a passenger than it is to ignore the people who you live with after the passenger is gone.

The second reason is simpler. Because most passengers will not complain, those who do are easily labeled as "too demanding" or "too picky." Rather than their complaint or concern being taken seriously, these passengers are viewed as the problem. All future interactions with the passenger are viewed through that label. I had an experience on an ultraluxury line where staff justified giving poor service by labeling my partner and me as "difficult passengers." They told managers that those passengers (us) simply "got what they deserved." Corporate managers "bought" the label. They dismissed a threatening telephone call made to our cabin by a member of the dining room staff, forgave a maitre d' who raised his voice to us, and initially refused to deal with me. I was only taken seriously following correspondence with the board of directors of the cruise line's parent company.

The list of unexpected problems can range from the severe, such as a sexual assault, to a minor nuisance, such as a waiter providing unacceptable service. It is impractical to try to provide a comprehensive list — you could always find one more item to add. But what's interesting here is how cruise lines handle complaints; responses vary widely and are often inconsistent. At times it even seems that cruise lines work against their own interests in dealing with problems.

Rather than try to summarize the range of things that can go wrong, and the likely responses, it may be more instructive to look at several items from the media, chosen in part because they illustrate the cruise industry's attitude about problems brought to them by their customers. Some of the cases are extreme, but that makes them that much more instructive.

Sorry, Your Clothes Have Been Incinerated

In 1997 a couple traveling on a Royal Caribbean Cruise Line vessel handed £1,000 (about $1,650) worth of dirty laundry to the cabin steward. They were later told that their clothes had been accidentally incinerated. After several months of correspondence following the cruise, "the couple were told that the ship's insurance limited compensation payments to £92 [$150] per person."[5] A local newspaper intervened on behalf of the couple, but to the best of my knowledge the outcome was never reported.

Your Injury Isn't Our Fault — Talk to Our Lawyer

In December 1996 Baseball Hall-of-Famer Eddie Mathews had an accident while vacationing on Carnival Cruise Line. In January 1998 he filed a lawsuit against the company claiming he had been permanently disabled after falling from one of the cruise line's tenders (the lifeboats used to transport passengers to and from the ship while anchored at port).

> Mathews broke a hip, fractured his spine and had more than one stroke as a result of the accident which happened when the tender moved away just as Mathews was stepping on to a pier in Grand Cayman. Mathews promptly fell between the pier and the tender and, while hanging between them, was crushed when the tender swung back towards him.[6]

Carnival defended itself by alleging the accident was Mathew's fault. Eddie Mathews died February 18, 2001, before the case went to court. Family members suggest he never completely recovered from the accident in 1996.

You Expected Air Conditioning?

Several cruises with deplorable conditions aboard Norwegian Cruise Line's *Norwegian Star* led to a class-action lawsuit in early 1998. The problems with the *Star* became public after passengers on the Thanksgiving cruise complained about plumbing and that air conditioning problems had forced them to sleep outdoors. Passengers from previous cruises with similar complaints joined in the class-action suit. Another group was added to the lawsuit after the same problems surfaced again with the Christmas cruise. The lack of air conditioning had again forced most passengers to sleep on deck. At the last minute, the ship's New Year cruise was canceled.

At the heart of the lawsuit is the fact that Norwegian Cruise Line has offered passengers a free cruise as compensation. The passengers are asking for a complete refund.[7] They are so close but yet so far; no resolution has been reported.

But Grandpa Is Missing!

Shortly after midnight on December 15, 1998, Royal Caribbean International's *Monarch of the Seas* struck a shoal off Philipsburg, St. Maarten. The impact tore a gash in the side of the ship and prompted a call to evacuate.

A couple rushed to their muster station, leaving the ashes of the man's grandfather behind in their cabin. They had intended to scatter the ashes in Barbados where the grandfather had been born. When Royal Caribbean later sent staff to the cabins to pack up passenger belongings and transfer them to shore, they returned with everything except the ashes. The box of ashes had disappeared. The cruise line's spokesperson "said that he did not believe the company would be liable for the loss of the ashes. Before they board cruise ships, passengers sign forms releasing the company from claims for lost goods."[8] Grandpa was gone, but not forgotten.

Don't Ask Us to Be Sensitive

On December 26, 1997, a 19-year-old woman drowned in a shipboard pool that was supposed to be closed for the night. According to the woman's family, the pool should have been covered (per company policy), a failure in the lighting system had prevented would-be rescuers from seeing if someone was in the pool, and the cruise line had handled the matter in a stressful manner. The ship's officers asked the family several times whether the young woman had been drinking and why she had been swimming alone.

Next, shortly after the body had been found, "the head of security for the cruise line asked the family to sign a statement that released the company from liability. When family members refused, the head of security became upset."[9] Cruise line officials then claimed that the young woman had been diving when diving wasn't allowed, but that was refuted later by an eyewitness, an employee of the ship.

The family is suing Holland America line for $1 million in the death of Erica Cummings, although even if they win the amount of the reward may be greatly restricted. According to an 80-year-old law called the Death on the High Seas Act, "if a death occurs more than three miles from US territory, the victim's relatives can seek economic recovery only for the loss of support to themselves, even if the operators of the ship committed an egregious act that caused the person's death."[10] In effect, the cruise line has no liability.

Gray Power 1, NCL 0

In March 2001 a California court denied a motion by Norwegian Cruise Line to dismiss a class-action complaint filed by 38 senior citizens who contend they missed a July 2000 Alaska cruise because the cruise line had booked their air travel. The seniors claim they missed the cruise because of the tight connection time allowed by the cruise line. The problem was foreseeable and had been brought to the attention of the cruise line's air/sea representative beforehand, but she responded that NCL "reserves that right to choose the air carrier, routing and city airport." According to a travel industry publication, the cruise line "would not reissue or exchange the air tickets."[11]

On the day of the cruise, the senior citizens arrived at the airport to find that their flight had been canceled. There wasn't sufficient time to make alternative flight arrangements and make it to the ship, so they missed the cruise. When they turned to their travel insurance issued by the cruise line, they were told the insurance did not cover their situation. They are suing Norwegian Cruise Line, which has agreed to put the senior citizens on another cruise within a year. The senior citizens simply want a refund.

Now Children, Behave Yourselves or Else

In May 2001 a British couple embarked on a two-month trip with Renaissance Cruises. Ten days before the end of the cruise, they were kicked off the ship in the British Virgin Islands for inciting a mutiny.

When the couple booked their trip, they were guaranteed that the price wouldn't fall. Once they were on the ship, they found that the amounts passengers had paid for the cruise differed widely. What they thought was a good deal was not, in fact, as good a deal as others had gotten. In frustration and anger, the husband prepared a one-page leaflet with "Are you entitled to a large refund on your cruise?" in bold printing across the top. The leaflet asked passengers to write their names, addresses, telephone numbers, cabin numbers, and the price they had paid for the cruise. Anyone who didn't fill out and return the information would not be part of a class-action lawsuit challenging Renaissance's pricing practices.

When the husband went to have the leaflet printed, the attendant made a copy and sent it to the captain. The man, who had not yet distributed the leaflet, was then summoned to the captain's office and told "that he had been 'actively engaged in the solicitation of our guests to participate in a class action suit' against the cruise line. [He] ... was told he must 'cease and desist' because it was a violation of the terms and conditions of the ticket."[12] The next day he was given a second letter and ordered off the ship. The man's wife "complained that she shouldn't have been punished with her husband. 'I wasn't involved in that letter, but just because I was his wife they I said I had to go as well.' "[13]

The man considered suing the cruise line for being "dumped" in the British Virgin Islands. However, maritime lawyers point out that he would have a tough time, given that cruise passengers agree to adhere to cruise line regulations when they buy their tickets. As well, when at sea the captain is in charge and has wide authority. He can do whatever is judged necessary for the safety and security of his ship.

An Exercise in Futility

In May 2000 my partner and I took a cruise on the *Radisson Diamond*. We experienced a minor problem that was a source of concern because we had a cruise booked on another Radisson ship several months later and didn't want to repeat the situation.

The first morning, music around the pool was too loud and included much that, given the makeup of passengers seated in the area, was inappropriate: rap and hard rock. Every hour or so, I, as well as others, asked the bartender to turn the music down, and it was. But each time a new bartender took over, again the music would be turned up, and again a request would be made to reduce the volume. This pattern repeated itself, day after day. One morning a passenger brought his own CDs and asked that they be played, ostensibly to get a break from the bartenders' choice of music.

The situation escalated when a bartender began saying under his breath every time he saw me, "Turn down the music?" He even made the comment one night at dinner while serving my wine at the staff captain's table.

After I spoke to his supervisors about the problem, his comments stopped, but he became passive-aggressive. One evening my partner went to the area around a bar to have an after-dinner cigarette. The bar was closed and she was the only one there. It was perfectly quiet — until I arrived to join her. Immediately, the bartender, who was cleaning the bar, turned the music on, loud enough to be bothersome.

We again spoke with onboard management but found that each time we complained, the passive-aggressive behavior became more intrusive and troublesome. We had to resign ourselves to remaining captive to the musical tastes of the bartenders.

When we returned home, we wrote to the company's chief executive officer. He sent two certificates for $250 off a future cruise but gave no assurance that what we had experienced was inconsistent with company policy. Apparently he couldn't understand that discount certificates are worthless if a company can't assure a passenger that the advertised product will be delivered. My second letter received a response described by my travel agency as arrogant.

I made one more attempt to clarify company policy before canceling our next cruise. I clearly asked the CEO whether we should expect unwanted music on our next cruise and how best to deal with a staff person who is rude or abusive. His response indicated that yes, we would be subjected to unwanted music. It also suggested that we shouldn't expect management to be able to deal with problematic staff.

In disbelief that a company would take this position, I wrote to the chief executive officer of the parent company to Radisson Seven Seas Cruises: the Carlson Companies. Although she did not respond, we did receive another letter from Radisson Seven Seas' CEO. In that letter he essentially called us liars, saying that we hadn't given the company a chance to resolve the problem on the *Diamond* because we hadn't notified staff or management, and he claimed that the bartenders have no ability to control the music around the pool. I responded with a letter that documented the close to two dozen complaints made to bartenders, the bar manager, and the food and beverage manager. I also pointed out his misinformation about the way his own ship is being run.

I did not receive a direct response to that letter, but my travel agency — a member of the Carlson Family of Companies — was told I am not welcome to return to Radisson Seven Seas Cruises.

WHAT CAN BE DONE?

THIS BOOK BEGAN WITH THE QUESTION of whether the cruise industry is socially and environmentally sustainable. Based on what you have just read, the answer would have to be no, in its current state the cruise industry is not. Problems range from misrepresentation of the cruise product to safety and security at sea, from assaults on the environment to assaults on workers. The question of What can be done? can be answered on at least two levels: what the cruise industry can do and what you as a consumer can do.

WHAT CAN THE CRUISE INDUSTRY DO?

Solutions to most issues discussed in this book are under the control of the cruise industry. The cruise lines choose how to advertise their product and whether to be forthright about what is and what is not included in a cruise fare. Although the industry is likely to say that passengers choose to spend extra money — they have it within their control not to — the simple fact is that some of the added expenses are unexpected and others are out of line.

Honesty about Money Grabs

Take gratuities, for example. Except for a few ultraluxury cruise lines, almost all cruise lines instruct passengers to pay gratuities and suggest the amounts to be given. Princess Cruises and Norwegian Cruise Line go as far as automatically charging tips to a passenger's onboard account. Why are these not collected upfront with the cruise fare? The answer is simple. If they were, the price of a one-week cruise would increase by at least $70, which may be a deterrent for many people, either because a land-based alternative is cheaper or because the price is pushed beyond a comfort level. By having the tips paid separately, the perceived price of a cruise is kept down.

Although I haven't thought much about the expectation of tips, I have always been struck by the difference between a cruise ship and a land-based resort. Whether all-inclusive or not, a hotel never creates the expectation or recommends that passengers should tip the staff. A cruise line could easily resolve a number of issues by including tips in the cruise fare. It would alleviate problems associated with the onboard mafia, provide the potential for reasonable salaries, and eliminate "tip night," which is usually the last night of the cruise and a hassle for both passengers and workers.

Cruise lines can similarly be more honest about onboard money grabs. Although I might argue the list has gotten much too long, my real concern is the degree to which passengers are unaware of the amount of extra spending that is common on a cruise ship. In addition, cruise lines have made it difficult to avoid some of their money grabs.

The prohibition against passengers bringing onboard their own beverages is a good example. The whole thing is foolish: my sister-in-law inquired about bringing bottled water onboard a Carnival Cruise Line ship and was told she could not; she'd have to purchase it onboard. I understand the reason for the prohibition — money — but I don't understand the logic. I have never had a hotel inspect my hand luggage to ensure I wasn't bringing beverages into my room, nor check my shopping bags every time I returned to the hotel from outside. Yet that is exactly what the hotel department on a cruise ship does.

Security and Safety

Several issues relate to security and safety. The safety of the ship is largely under the control of the cruise line. It chooses whether to allocate the staff required by its own operational manuals, and it defines the hours of work and of rest had by those on the bridge and in other work settings. That fatigue is a major factor in shipboard accidents and injuries reflects a problem with the system. The problem is easily fixed, but it has financial implications. It is also contrary to the wave in the industry toward having ships with more passengers and fewer staff.

Physical safety and security of passengers may be a more thorny problem, but still not insurmountable. Cases of sexual assault suggest that it needs to be made clear to workers that rapes and other assaults will not be tolerated. As well, given the closed setting of a cruise ship, it may be worth the investment to have a counselor onboard a ship, available to both passengers and crew.

The counselor would be someone competent in dealing with cases of sexual assault, who could serve as an ombudsperson in matters arising between passengers and staff or between shipboard employees. If a counselor is to be effective and seen as someone to turn to, it is essential that he or she be independent of the ship's hierarchical structure — a status similar to the ship's physician, who on medical matters essentially answers to no one onboard, not even the captain. Counselors would need to be independent, and independently available. The simple fact is that abuses are known to occur on ships, but the information is kept within the shipboard community. The only way that information gets out is by having an outsider brought in.

Safety from illness can also be improved. Cruise line galleys should be more vigilant in following guidelines for food preparation and storage, and ships generally must take greater responsibility for sanitation and cleanliness. The fact that a cruise line can be consistently cited by the Vessel Sanitation Program of the Centers for Disease Control (CDC) for the same deficiencies on several of its ships suggests a weakness in the cruise company itself rather than a random case of oversight. A ship doing its job shouldn't be failing its sanitation inspection, and those that are cited for major deficiencies should not be passed with a perfect score.

Ships can similarly take more responsibility for cleanliness, including air vents. Although it shouldn't have been necessary, I had to request that fuzz, dust, and whatever was growing within be removed from the recessed light fixtures in my cabin on the *Radisson Diamond*. This was minimally taken care of, but the accumulation of "stuff" in the bathroom light fixture was left untouched. I have been in very few cabins on cruise ships that were comparable in cleanliness to an onshore hotel. Aside from the question of whether or not dust and other debris is a health risk, there is the issue that going on a cruise means often living in a room with dirt and debris that other people leave behind.

Although it seems incomprehensible, I once had a bathroom with dried blood speckled down the tile wall.

Medical care is another area in which certain cruise lines could greatly improve. All cruise lines should be clear about the nature and limitation of medical services available onboard. They should also be forthright about their policies regarding medical personnel. Passengers go on a cruise, never thinking twice about whether a doctor will be available and whether the doctor is qualified. Cruise lines should clearly state in their brochures the nature of their medical team, including the minimum qualifications of those hired. While that may not eliminate lapses in medical service, it would give passengers information that allows for an informed decision in choosing a cruise line. In addition, if minimum qualifications were not present, then the passenger would have greater recourse than is presently the case.

Environmental Protection

Despite all the hype about being environmentally responsible and environmentally friendly, the environment remains one area in which the cruise industry has considerable room for improvement. The industry has not demonstrated that it takes the environment seriously, nor has it acted voluntarily. The first statement by the International Council of Cruise Lines (ICCL) on environmental issues coincided with the plea agreement between the US Justice Department and Royal Caribbean International in 1999. The second statement, issued two years later, included environmental standards for cruise ships and coincided with the final stage of the Alaska Senate's consideration of legislation that would monitor the industry and enforce environmental standards. Rather than welcoming this sort of development, the cruise industry has resisted attempts to produce greater environmental responsibility.

If the industry wanted to make a positive impression, it could unilaterally announce measurable environmental standards, more stringent than the minimum allowed under the International Convention for the Prevention of Pollution from Ships (MARPOL), which would be certified, monitored, and enforced.

If the hype were more than just hype, this would be an infinitely sensible way to proceed. Instead, the cruise industry's approach appears to be one of deploying clean ships where environmental standards are enforced and sending other ships to areas without enforcement. To live up to its pronouncements about environmental responsibility, I believe the industry needs to do more than the minimum provided by international regulations. Wouldn't it be wonderful if cruise lines were, as they sometimes label themselves, actually leaders in the environmental movement? They have the technology and the ability, but do they have the will?

Worker Issues

In its independent study on the shipping industry published in 2000, the International Commission on Shipping (ICONS) exhaustively considered the issue of workers. The report *Ships, Slaves, and Competition* summarizes the problem as "including long hours of work, disadvantageous contractual and pay arrangements, significant national discrimination in the lengths of crew contracts, prevention of access by seafarer missions and unions and lack of safety training for hotel staff. The worst examples of questionable company employment practices for cruise ships relate to the North American market. Most of these vessels, while not US flagged, carry US passengers, operate out of US ports and visit ports in the Caribbean. A considerable number also visit ports on Canada's East and West coasts."[1]

The commission recommended that the US government:

> (i) acknowledge the extensive exploitation of seafarers serving on US port-based cruise ships and ensure that minimum standards of decent work as contained in the ILO [International Labour Organization] Convention No. 147 are applied; and
> (ii) ensure that representatives from seafarers' missions, welfare organizations and unions have free on board access to crew members.[2]

These recommendations provide clear direction.

Part of the problem is that crew members, like passengers, are not given full knowledge about what to expect when they step onboard a cruise ship. Take, for example, "Magdalena Norkowska of Warsaw, Poland, [who] was attracted by claims she could make

$2,000 a month in salary and tips as a bartender and waitress aboard the *Horizon*, a Celebrity Cruise Line ship. The hours turned out to be longer than promised, and the pay less by half."[3] Her experience is not uncommon.

A further problem is sexual assaults of both male and female employees. The presence of a counselor or ombudsperson might assist in bringing this information forward and having the situation dealt with. I know that what goes on aboard a cruise ship is unsurprising to the people working on and managing the ship. But it might be quite a surprise to the cruise line's onshore management. Without bold, independent action, the abuses will continue and workers will continue to be exploited and oppressed.

Dealing Honestly with Customers

The cruise industry has done much to create an image of being concerned about its customers. Holland America Line has a "Guest Relations Manager" on each of its ships; Royal Caribbean International and Celebrity Cruises both have a "Vice-President of Total Guest Satisfaction." However, the behavior of these companies is often inconsistent with the labels given their staff. I have listened many times while an irate passenger met with the guest relations manager and have consistently been amazed at how little training these folks have in how to deal with people. As is often the case with the cruise lines' response to letters of complaint, there is very little indication that a passenger's concerns are heard. Very often the interaction ends with the passenger simply resigning themselves to the situation.

For all of their talk about concern for their customer, cruise lines could learn to simply listen to what customers are telling them. While most customers simply want to be sure that their concern or problem has been heard, the corporate attitude is one of "us versus them," an attitude which precludes listening and often relies on explaining why things are the way that they are. Even when a concern is heard, the customer relations folks at cruise lines have an uncanny tendency to write letters that end with a statement of how great the cruise line is, expressing confidence that the passenger will experience this when he or she returns for another cruise. This statement is made no matter how horrible a past cruise has been.

This is sad because cruise lines spend so much money trying to attract the first-time cruiser. But they do very little to keep the customers that they have by addressing even minor lapses.

WHAT CAN *YOU* DO?

In an ideal world, it would be enough to identify what is needed from the industry, which would then respond accordingly. However, the above recommendations, no matter how reasonable, are unlikely to produce changes within the industry. Effecting change requires direct action by individuals and by groups.

Educate

The easiest and most effective means of influencing the industry is through education. The cruise industry is sensitive to public opinion and perceptions; they will be motivated to take corrective action when the underside of the industry is brought into daylight.

Part of this effort can be directed to the general public, including anyone who is thinking of going on a cruise. In my experience, the biggest surprises are that "all-inclusive" does not really mean all-inclusive, that there is incongruity between cruises as advertised and cruises as reality, and that cruise ships are not as safe as most people believe them to be. The public has little awareness about accidents at sea and is often dumbfounded to learn about sexual assaults onboard cruise ships.

Education can also be more focused. Many members of labor organizations are unaware of the plight of workers on cruise ships — you can make them aware. Likewise, many environmentalists overlook the cruise industry as a source of pollution. They don't see the smokestack out their window, but the harm to the environment is still there. They, too, will benefit from information sharing.

There are others who need information. Parents welcome information about the risk to their children onboard a cruise ship. Women welcome being made aware of the risk of harassment or assault. And everyone appreciates being forewarned about the risk of foodborne and other illnesses.

Cruise Ship Blues contains much information; share what you have learned with others. One form of effective action is to see that those needing the information receive it. Talk to people, give or lend them a copy of the book, but make them aware. Some may use the knowledge for their personal vacation decisions; others may use it for personal or collective action. This is how a grass-roots movement is born, which realistically can happen with modest efforts.

Advocate

Advocacy can take a number of forms. For example, given the history of the US Congress and the cruise industry, you might find out your congressperson's and senator's position on issues related to the cruise industry. You can advocate positions on current legislation, but also advocate more generally for changes in environmental laws, labor laws, and tax laws under which the industry operates. As for tax laws, it can be as simple as "I pay taxes, you pay taxes; why don't they pay taxes?" Make yourself aware of the issues and let your voice be heard.

Labor issues are another area for advocacy. Labor unions are committed to worker issues and share a sense of solidarity with workers on cruise ships. You can advocate in a local union for boycotts of the cruise industry and work to make this an issue that goes beyond the local. Or you can advocate for a boycott, working independently of a labor organization. Anyone can put together a group, provide information, and advocate for social responsibility.

If you live in a coastal state or province, you can advocate within the state or provincial legislature. A number of states, including Florida, Hawaii, and California, are considering action to better monitor and regulate the cruise industry, particularly concerning the environment. Support these efforts and do what you can to advocate others to lend their support. For example, under 2000 state legislation, California implemented an inter-agency task force to make recommendations for reducing cruise ship pollution; a final report is due in 2003. Monitor the work of the task force and advocate for recommendations you agree with. Similar initiatives are being undertaken, or should be undertaken, in other coastal states. You can be a catalyst or a supporter.

People living in port cities can take an interest in the impact of the cruise industry on their own harbor. Learn about the environmental impact of cruise ships, and advocate for local efforts to monitor cruise ships and prevent pollution. It isn't just what a ship does in the harbor — for example, in 2001 Carnival Cruise Line admitted in its first quarterly report to the California Cruise Ship Environmental Task Force that it had regularly discharged 40,000 gallons of graywater each time it was docked at the San Pedro Cruise terminal in Los Angeles between January and May of that year. Think also about what happens at sea — about the stream of effluent that can be left in a ship's wake as it passes beyond the 3-mile and 12-mile point from your coastline.

Participate

There are already a number of organizations concerned with issues related to the cruise industry. You might find that your limited available time means that your best efforts are in supporting an existing group or organization. There is no need to create a group when there are already those that can use your support — economic, moral, and physical.

Environmental Organizations

Two environmental groups have projects focused specifically on the cruise industry.

1. **The Bluewater Network Cruise Ship Campaign**
   311 California Street, Suite 510, San Francisco, CA 94104
   ph: (415) 544-0790 fax: (415) 544-0796
   www.bluewaternetwork.org

The Bluewater Network's Cruise Ship Campaign has had some notable success. On March 17, 2000, it filed a petition with the Environmental Protection Agency (EPA) to address a number of issues related to pollution by cruise ships; 58 organizations signed on to the petition. The EPA responded by launching a major initiative to assess the volumes, characteristics, and environmental impacts of cruise ship wastes, the effectiveness of existing regulatory and nonregulatory programs for managing these wastes, and options for their better environmental management. The outcome of the process will be recommendations for how to deal with pollution from cruise ships. In the meantime, the Bluewater Network is exploring with the EPA an eco-labeling program for cruise ships that would indicate those ships meeting an agreed-upon minimum standard for environmental protection.

In 2001 the Bluewater Network settled a court case forcing the EPA to regulate air pollution from big ships, including cruise ships. Since most cruise ships are foreign-flagged and the new rules will probably exempt foreign ships, the Bluewater Network expects to again have to sue the EPA, or alternatively to introduce legislation in Congress to capture foreign ships.

The California Cruise Ship Environmental Task Force was formed in January 2001 under legislation sponsored by the Bluewater Network. The task force monitors the cruise industry's impact on California's environment and makes determinations on the adequacy of existing regulations for cruise ship waste management.

The Bluewater Network is actively involved in regulatory advocacy, in lobbying Congress and state legislatures in California and Alaska, in public education, and in litigation.

2. **Oceans Blue Foundation Cruise Ship Stewardship Initiative**
    405 - 134 Abbott Street, Vancouver, BC, V6B 2K4 Canada
    ph: (604) 684-2583 fax: (604) 684-6942
    www.oceansblue.org

Founded in Vancouver, Canada, in 1996, the Oceans Blue Foundation is a nonprofit environmental organization working to conserve coastal environments through responsible and sustainable tourism. It operates in the USA and Canada. The Oceans Blue Foundation was the first organization in North America to focus on developing and promoting best practices and standards for all sectors of the tourism industry.

The Cruise Ship Stewardship Initiative, the foundation's latest project, directly supports environmental protection efforts in Alaska and Canada, and seeks similar regulation and control of cruise ship emissions in Canada and beyond. The organization is presently working with a number of partners on developing a scheme for eco-certification (similar to the Bluewater Network's eco-labeling program) of cruise ships, and is exploring other strategies for preserving the coastal environment.

There are other useful organizations as well. For example, West Coast Environmental Law (www.wcel.org), a public interest environmental law group, has produced a comprehensive review and analysis of local, federal, and international regulations relating to ship emissions. It is actively involved in efforts to form policies that protect the environment. The Earth Island Institute (www.earthisland.org), through its Campaign to Protect America's Waters, has been directly involved in Alaska's efforts to regulate the cruise industry, as well as in efforts beyond Alaska. Like many other environmental groups, the Earth Island Institute's concerns include issues related to the cruise industry.

Labor Issues

Becoming involved in labor issues is less straightforward. The main organization involved with worker issues is the Seafarers' Section of the International Transport Workers' Federation (ITF — www.itf.org.uk). Based in London, the Seafarers' Section focuses on the rights of workers on all ships and is actively engaged in a campaign to end the use of flags of convenience. Its cruise ship campaign is focused on educating workers of their rights and on having and enforcing collective agreements on cruise ships. The Seafarers Trust has, several times in the past couple of years, assisted cruise ships workers who were left stranded with back-pay owed and no means to return home.

For people living in port cities, there is some opportunity for direct activity. Most ports have a seafarer's mission, often sponsored by religious organizations and supported by the ITF. These missions provide a way for you to learn about the cruise industry and the plight of its workers, as well as an opportunity to volunteer your time and resources. Going to and spending time at the mission is one of the few opportunities many of us will have to deal directly with the cruise industry in the form of a real person in a real situation.

Organize

For those with the time, there is plenty opportunity to organize collective action. I have already mentioned opportunities for advocating labor unions to take an interest in their brethren on cruise ships. It may be easier than it appears to gain the support of union locals for a petition addressing the plight of workers on cruise ships. And there are other opportunities to help, whether you live in a landlocked area or a port area.

You might consider informational pickets or leafleting. Either one can be a way to educate people about the cruise industry. They can advocate a boycott of cruise ships or simply make people aware of necessary precautions, should they be thinking about a cruise. There are other methods as well for collectively distributing information.

Consider organizing a collective campaign to alert parents and women to the safety risks on a cruise ship. This can focus on a neighborhood, a town or city, or a larger area. The scale of the effort is less important than getting information to those who need it.

There are many more possibilities for organizing and other action. Groups and individuals subjecting the cruise industry to critical analysis and attention are rather new, so the landscape is still relatively clear of well-entrenched efforts and organizations. This may be intimidating to some people in that there is no place to immediately plug into, but to others the opportunities to build grassroots actions and movements, and to see them have an impact, can be exciting.

There is also opportunity for creativity. In January 2002 the town of Yakutat, Alaska, sent a bill for $382,833 to cruise lines whose ships traverse Disenchantment Bay.

> The tax is unprecedented because ships do not dock in Yakatut. But the vessels enter scenic Disenchantment Bay in borough waters to show passengers Hubbard Glacier.... Yukatut residents who hunt seals worry that ships are hurting seal populations in the bay.... Civic leaders also say ill passengers traveling through borough waters have taken a toll on city medical services.[4]

The cruise industry expressed its desire to negotiate an alternative to the tax, fearing that the levy would incite similar taxes by other cities along cruise routes.

Major impacts on the cruise industry may be slow to realize, but as public awareness of the problems increase and as reservations for cruises fall off, the industry is likely to fall in line. Cruise lines are in business to make money; a decrease in their resource base — that is, paying passengers — will result in the companies reacting in ways to expand it. My hope is that any expansion will be built upon greater responsibility for the safety and security of passengers, on environmental responsibility and integrity, and on proper and humane treatment of workers.

I STILL WANT TO TAKE A CRUISE

You may still want to take a cruise and wonder whether one cruise line is better than the others. That assessment is difficult to make. Without a system of certification regarding labor and environmental practices, there is no formal mechanism — as there is, to some extent, with a ship's sanitation — for learning what a cruise line is doing and how well they are doing it. As we have seen often, cruise lines project an image such as environmental responsibility, and then after the fact, reports contradicting that image emerge.

In the absence of any formal certification schemes or reliable assessments, my website at www.cruisejunkie.com may provide some useful information and direction. The noncommercial site is regularly updated with links to reports, investigations, and new developments regarding labor, ship safety and security, and the environment. The site will not tell you which cruise line to choose, but it can provide insight into different companies and their practices. It also reports on development of any certification or similar schemes regarding environmental and labor practices, and in terms of ship safety and security.

I also main a comprehensive website of links to cruise lines, ports, commercial and personal pages, and concessionaires and suppliers. That site (www.ucs.mun.ca/~rklein/cruise.html), also entirely noncommercial, will direct you to most of the major (and many obscure but useful) cruise resources on the Internet. It is a useful place to begin if you are just starting your exploration of the cruise industry and cruising on the Internet.

APPENDIX A:
MISHAPS AT SEA

January 2000 — December 2001

Carnival Cruise Line

Date	Ship	Details of Mishap
Jan 00	*Celebration*	Fire in generator. Ship adrift for 6 hours; no toilets or air conditioning
Feb 00	*Destiny*	Propulsion problems. Ship adrift for 27 hours
May 00	*Destiny*	Mechanical difficulties. 1 cruise canceled; the next delayed 1 day and sails at slower speeds
July 00	*Paradise*	Malfunction of propulsion system as leaving port. Cruise canceled; next 3 cruises also canceled
Sep 00	*Victory*	Hits New York City pier. Damage to pier; ship proceeds
Oct 00	*Elation*	Preventative maintenance of propulsion system. 2 cruises canceled
Aug 01	*Inspiration*	Strikes barge in Mississippi River — undamaged

Celebrity Cruises

Date	Ship	Details of Mishap
July 00	*Millennium*	Engine and plumbing problems. Stop at Stockholm skipped; goes to Germany for repairs
Nov 00	*Millennium*	Propulsion problems. 4 cruises canceled
Feb 01	*Millennium*	Drydocked to repair propulsion problems
Jun 01	*Galaxy*	Damaged propeller leaving Amsterdam. Cruise canceled
Jun 01	*Infinity*	Drydocked to repair propulsion problems

Festival Cruises (First European Cruises)

Date	Ship	Details of Mishap
Feb 01	*Mistral*	Grounded off Nevis. Stuck for more than 1 day
Aug 01	*European Vision*	Propulsion problems. Cruise canceled mid way
Aug 01	*Mistral*	Propulsion malfunction. Cruise cut short

Golden Sun Cruises

Date	Ship	Details of Mishap
Jun 00	*Aegean Spirit*	Fuel leak in port at Iraklion, Crete. Ship repaired and cruise continues
July 01	*Arcadia*	Detained for health violations
July 01	*Ocean Glory I*	Detained for safety and health violations

Holland America Line

Date	Ship	Details of Mishap
Apr 00	*Rotterdam*	Hit by rogue wave. Damage to any thing not bolted down; rough seas for Pacific crossing
May 00	*Nieuw Amsterdam*	Fire in crew quarters while in Glacier Bay. Cruise delayed 12 hours awaiting Coast Guard clearance[1]
Oct 00	*Veendam*	Electrical generator failure — no power for 3 hours
Jun 01	*Zaandam*	Discovered that sprinkler heads in some rooms not connected to water supply

Norwegian Cruise Line

Date	Ship	Details of Mishap
May 01	*Norway*	Cruise canceled due to safety violations — 106 leaks in fire sprinkler system
May 01	*Norwegian Sky*	Autopilot malfunction causes roll. 70+ passengers injured, 16 hospitalized
Sep 01	*Norway*	Grounded; collides with pier at New York City. No damage to ship

Premier Cruises

Date	Ship	Details of Mishap
Jan 00	*Island Breeze*	Problems with boilers. Cruise delayed 2 days
Mar 00	*Seabreeze*	Engine boiler breakdown. Cruise canceled
May 00	*Big Red Boat III*	Leaves port with anchor down; strikes under water power lines. Power out for 17 hours at Newport, RI. Cruise continues
Jun 00	*Big Red Boat II*	Maiden voyage canceled at last minute due to unfinished renovations
Jun 00	*Big Red Boat II*	Problems with air conditioning, plumbing, and propulsion. 2 cruises canceled
Jun 00	*Island Breeze*	Collision with tugboat — damaged propeller, tug sinks. 2 cruises canceled
July 00	*Rembrandt*	Air-conditioning problems on multiple cruises
July 00	*Seabreeze*	Engine problems. Ship adrift for 14 hours
Aug 00	*Big Red Boat II*	Elevator malfunction at end of cruise. Passengers kept onboard for several hours at port
Dec 00	*Sea Breeze*	Sunk in 30-foot seas in the Atlantic. No passengers aboard at the time; no injuries

P&O Princess

Date	Ship	Details of Mishap
May 00	*Aurora*	Problem with overheated propeller shaft 18 hours into maiden voyage. Cruise canceled
Sep 00	*Oriana*	Hit by 40-foot wave — smashed windows in 6 cabins; 20 cabins flooded. 6 people injured; cruise delayed
Dec 00	*Crown Princess*	Loss of generator power. Sails at reduced speed
Mar 01	*Regal Princess*	Grounded at Cairns. Ship freed and continues
Apr 01	*Dawn Princess*	Engine problems. 5 hours late in arriving at Barbados
Apr 01	*Royal Princess*	Breaks loose from mooring at Port Said, Egypt; drifts into path of cargo ship. Minor damage
Jun 01	*Crown Princess*	Mechanical breakdown; towed to Copenhagen. Delayed at Stockholm for 3 days

July 01   *Pacific Sky*   Hits major storm. Cuts and bruises to passengers; docks 36 hours late

Royal Caribbean International

Date	Ship	Details of Mishap
Oct 00	*Grandeur of the Seas*	Loss of electrical power — towed to port. Delayed 12 hours
Dec 00	*Sovereign of the Seas*	Partial loss of electrical power. Cruise ends at Port Canaveral and passengers bused to Port Everglades; next cruise canceled
Apr 01	*Radiance of the Seas*	Hits heavy seas — balcony cabins, Seaview and Windjammer cafés flooded
Jun 01	*Nordic Prince*	Engine room fire, loss of power. Passengers return to Bermuda and fly home
Oct 01	*Nordic Empress*	Damaged at pier during storm. Departure delayed; next cruise canceled

Sun Cruises (Airtours)

Date	Ship	Details of Mishap
Feb 00	*Carousel*	Runs over rocks; propeller damage and oil leak — a 50-ton spill. Abandon ship
Feb 00	*Sundream*	Failing generators; no air conditioning and limited power for 2 days. Similar problems the previous week[2]

Others

Date	Ship	Details of Mishap
Jan 00	*Olympic Countess*	Engine problems. Passengers transferred to the Triton and continue
Feb 00	*Clipper Adventurer*	Trapped in ice jam off Antarctica; freed by icebreaker. No damage; 24-hour delay
Apr 00	*Ocean Explorer*	Engine failure. World cruise ended
May 00	*Riviera I*	Ship seized for failure to pay fuel bills. Passengers stranded in Tahiti
May 00	*World Discoverer*	Hits rock or a reef and holed — forced to beach. 100 passengers rescued from Solomon Islands
July 00	*Funchal*	Loss of power. Cruise canceled

July 00	*QE 2*	Collides in 3-ship incident at New York harbor; scrapes and dents only
Oct 00	*Regal Empress*	Mechanical failure. Anchored for a few hours to make repairs
Oct 00	*Universe Explorer*	Collides with container vessel; repairs made without delay
Dec 00	*Seabourn Sun*	Propeller damaged. Several cruises canceled
Dec 00	*Stella Solaris*	Engine problems. Ship pulled from service for 3 months
Feb 01	*Bremen*	Hit by rogue wave — wheelhouse windows break and water enters bridge. Detour to Montevideo for repairs
Feb 01	*Patriot*	Engine problems. Cruise canceled
Mar 01	*Caledonian Star*	Damaged by large wave in storm; guided to port by Argentinean Navy
May 01	*Wilderness Explorer*	Grounded in Alaska
Jun 01	*Costa Tropicale*	Grounded at Venice; towed free by tugboats. 2 weeks later, grounded again at Mykonos; towed free by Costa Atlantica
Jun 01	*Sheltered Seas*	Engine problems. Passengers evacuated
Jun 01	*Unnamed Swiss-registered riverboat*	Collision with freighter in Germany
Oct 01	*Regal Empress*	Detained in port for 1½ days by Coast Guard midway through cruise for safety deficiencies. 1 port of call canceled; cruise ends 6 hours late
Nov 01	*Arkona*	Runs into dock after engine room fire causes loss of power. Passengers flown home
Nov 01	*Asuka*	Collision with cargo ship off coast of Kobe. No injuries

ENDNOTES

The Inaugural Sail: An Introduction to the Cruise Industry

1 "Global Cruise Industry Tops 12M Passengers for First Time," *Lloyd's List* (May 4, 2001), <www.lloydslist.com>.

2 "Newbuildings League," *Seatrade Insider News* (February 26, 2002).

3 See Bernard D. Nossiter, "Cunard Cancels Ads after Unfavorable News Story," *Washington Post* (February 17, 1978), p. A31. The *Sunday Times* story reported the *Queen Elizabeth 2* had been serving mixed drinks with ice cubes that had previously been used to chill raw fish, carrying ice cubes in dirty drums, and running up a fecal coliform count in the ice that was too high to count. It also reported that a spring 1977 cruise on the *QE 2* had left 216 passengers with diarrhea.

4 Carnival Corporation's view is clearly expressed by Tim Gallagher (vice-president of public relations) in Ted B. Kissel, "The Deep Blue Greed," *Miami New Times* (February 3-9, 2000), <www.miaminewtimes.com>.

Chapter 1: Onboard the Floating Resort

1 Mike Beirne, "Renaissance Cruises Close to Naming New Agency," *Adweek News Wire* (July 17, 2001).

2 These amounts were provided to me by onboard managers. Figures cited by Bob Dickinson and Andy Vladimir in *Selling the Sea: An Inside Look at the Cruise Industry* (John Wiley and Sons, 1997) are a bit different. They suggest per diems of $8 to $11 on mass-market lines, $8 to $18 on premium lines, and $25 to $30 on ultraluxury lines. They estimate a restaurant or hotel would have to charge between $33 and $40 to provide what a cruise line provides at $10 a day.

3 Nancy Huie, "F&B Spending on the Rise," *Cruise Industry News Quarterly* (Fall 1995), p. 94.

4 Nancy Huie, "How to Control Food Costs," *Cruise Industry News Quarterly* (Winter 1995-96), pp. 92-93.

5 Michael Grossman, "The Cruise Industry in Retrospect," *Cruise Industry News Quarterly* (Summer 1995), p. 61.

6 A company press release dated April 24, 2001, stated that the "fine wines" on Seabourn Cruise Line's complimentary list included R.H. Phillips Chardonnay (California), Caliterra Chardonnay (Chile), Loraine Valley Pinot Noir (California), Merlot Aresti (Chile), and Shiraz-Cabernet Sauvignon Banrock Station (Australia).

Chapter 2: The Myth of the All-Inclusive Vacation

1　This story appeared in several newspapers. The original source is: Marc Lacey, "Cost of Cruise's Extras Could Leave You High and Dry," *Los Angeles Times* (September 14, 1997), p. L2.

2　Carnival Corporation press release, "Proposed Combination of Carnival and P&O Princess," *PR Newswire* (January 24, 2002).

3　Jon Ashworth, "A Ship That Thinks It's a Conference Centre," *London Times* (July 14, 2001), <www.thetimes.co.uk>.

4　See Michael Connor, "Norwegian Line Would Fit Nicely with Carnival," *Reuters* (December 2, 1999).

5　Ashworth, "A Ship That Thinks It's a Conference Centre."

6　Nancy Huie, "The Business of Shopping," *Cruise Industry News Quarterly* (Summer 1995), p. 50.

7　Rob Marjerison, "Maximizing Onboard Revenue," *Cruise Industry News Quarterly* (Winter 1995-96), p. 82.

8　Nancy Huie, "F&B Spending on the Rise," *Cruise Industry News Quarterly* (Fall 1995), p. 95.

9　Christopher Reynolds, "A Toast to Your Cruise! Now Hand over That Booze," *Los Angeles Times* (October 19, 1997), p. L2.

10　Christopher Reynolds, "Minor's Death Raises Issues of Drinking on Cruise Ships," *Los Angeles Times* (August 7, 1994), p. L2.

11　See Arline Bleeker, "Cruise Lines Adjust Rules on Booze Use," *Seattle Times* (January 20, 2002), <seattletimes.nwsource.com>.

12　Reynolds, "A Toast to Your Cruise!"

13　For a discussion of casinos, see Rosemary Clancy, "The Rise in Popularity of Casino Operations," *Cruise Industry News Quarterly* (Summer 1999), p. 38.

14　Marjerison, "Maximizing Onboard Revenue."

15　J. Norman Howard, "Cruising, Better than Ever?", *Cruise Industry News Quarterly* (Summer 1993), pp. 62-63.

16　Bruce Mohl and Patricia Wen, "Disappointed Couple Want Refund on Ring Bought in Mexico," *Boston Globe* (December 19, 1999), p. B2.

17　"Some Guarantee: Claim Denied — Despite Documentation," *Conde Nast Traveler* (December 1996), p. 70.

18　Mohl and Wen, "Disappointed Couple Want Refund."

19　On Celebrity Cruises' Millennium-class ships, a thalassotherapy pool is placed in an area that had been designed for free access. At one point, a sign at the entrance of the pool area stated something like "Spa Pool for Paying Spa Guests Only," and Celebrity charged $20 for admission. Following an uproar on the "rec.travel.cruises" Usenet newsgroup, the company issued a public message from the "Vice-President of Total Guest Satisfaction" in mid-July 2001 announcing it was discontinuing the charge.

20 For a comparative discussion of spas, see Edwin McDowell, "Shipboard Spas Are the New Wave," *New York Times* (February 4, 2001), <www.nytimes.com>.

21 See <www.steinerleisure.com/sea.html>.

22 See Steiner Limited press release, "Steiner Limited Agrees to Acquire a 60% Interest in Mandara Spa LLC and Mandara Spa Asia Ltd.," *PR Newswire* (June 27, 2001).

23 See Kitty Bean Yancey, "Cruise Lines Draw Profits from Selling Works of Art," *USA Today* (February 9, 2001), <www.usatoday.com>.

24 Kitty Bean Yancey, "Art Auctions at Sea Could Soak You," *USA Today* (February 9, 2001), <www.usatoday.com>.

25 See "Exclusive Destinations Concept an Economic Necessity for 1990s: Out-Islands the In-Thing," *Lloyd's List* (October 18, 1991), <www.lloydslist.com>.

26 See "On-board Revenue: Value for Money," *Cruise Industry News Quarterly* (Winter 1997-98), p. 30.

27 See Greg Miller, "In-Cabin Amenities," *Cruise Industry News Quarterly* (Summer 1996), p. 36.

28 See Greg Miller, "In-Cabin Amenities: Keeping Passengers Safe and Well-Fed," *Cruise Industry News Quarterly* (Summer 1998), p. 28.

29 See Christopher Reynolds, "Lawsuits Say Cruises Go Overboard with Port Fees," *Los Angeles Times* (July 28, 1996), p. L2. Also see "Cruise Lines Sued over Port Charges," *Los Angeles Times* Southland edition (April 25, 1996), p. D2, <www.latimes.com>.

30 Many cruise lines provided vouchers for discounts on future cruises as their settlement of claims of overcharges in port charges. Carnival Cruise Line, for example, issued 4.5 million vouchers worth $126 million toward future cruises. Vouchers ranged in value from $25 to $55, depending on the length of cruise taken. That lawsuit, filed in 1996, was finally settled in May 2001.

31 See Molly Morris, "VIPA Agrees to Crown Bay Dock Expansion," *St. Thomas Source* (August 15, 2001), <www.onesource.com/stthomasvi>.

32 Ibid.

33 Molly Morris, "VIPA, WICO, Chamber Share Views on Crown Bay," *St. Thomas Source* (December 17, 2001), <www.onesource.com/stthomasvi>.

34 See Molly Morris, "VIPA Decides to Develop Crown Bay on Its Own," *St. Thomas Source* (April 2, 2002), <www.onesource.com/stthomasvi>.

35 "Carnival in J/V to Build Port near Cancun," *Seatrade Insider News* (November 7, 2001).

Chapter 3: Beyond the Muster Drill

1 Testimony of Jim Hall (US National Transportation Safety Board chairperson) before the House Committee on Transportation and Infrastructure, Subcommittee on Coast Guard and Maritime

Transportation, regarding cruise ship safety, October 7, 1999, <http://www.house.gov/transportation/cgmt/10-07-99/hall.html>.

2   See, for example: National Transportation Safety Board, *Marine Accident Report: Fire on Board the Liberian Passenger Ship Ecstasy, Miami, Florida, July 20, 1998*, NTSB/MAR-01/01, 2001; and National Transportation Safety Board, *Marine Accident Brief Report: Fire on Board the Netherlands-Registered Passenger Ship Nieuw Amsterdam, Glacier Bay, Alaska, May 23, 2000*, NTSB/MBR-01/01, 2001.

3   See, for example: Transportation Safety Board of Canada, Marine Occurrence Report: *Grounding, Passenger Vessel "Hanseatic" Simpson Strait, Northwest Territories, August 29 1996*, (TSBC, 1996); US National Transportation Safety Board, *Marine Accident Report: Grounding of the Liberian Passenger Ship Star Princess, on Poundstone Rock, Lynn Canal, Alaska, June 23, 1995*, NTSB/MAR-97/02, 1997; National Transportation Safety Board, *Marine Accident Report Grounding of the Panamanian Passenger Ship* Royal Majesty, *on Rose and Crown Shoal near Nantucket, Massachusetts, June 10, 1995*, NTSB/MAR-97/01, 1997; National Transportation Safety Board, *Grounding of U.S. Passenger Vessel M/V Yorktown Clipper in Glacier Bay, Alaska, August 18, 1993*, NTSB/MAR-94/02, 1994; National Transportation Safety Board, *Grounding of the United Kingdom Passenger Vessel RMS* Queen Elizabeth 2 *near Cuttyhunk Island, Vineyard Sound, Massachusetts, August 7, 1992*, NTSB/MAR-93/01, 1993.

4   A full report on the 1989 collision of Carnival Cruise Line's *Celebration* with a Cuban cement freighter was not issued because the *Celebration*'s crew refused to cooperate with investigators. A partial report is contained in National Transportation Safety Board report no. DCA89MM029.

5   See National Transportation Safety Board, *Collision of the Netherlands Antilles Passenger Ship* Noordam *and the Maltese Bulk Carrier* Mount Ymitos *in the Gulf of Mexico, November 6, 1993*, NTSB/MAR-95/01, 1995.

6   See "Cruise Passengers Still Questioning Predawn Jolt," *Los Angeles Times* (June 28, 1997), p. B2.

7   See Transportation Safety Board of Canada, *Marine Occurrence Report M96W0187: Near Collision Between the Cruise Ship "Statendam" and the Tug/Barge Unit "Belleisle Sound"/"Radium 622," Discovery Passage, British Columbia, 11 August 1996* (TSBC, 1996).

8   See Sarah Boseley, "Passengers in Terror on Blazing Cruise Liner," *Manchester Guardian* (October 6, 1997), p. 1.

9   Brittany Wallman and Peter Bernard, "Coast Guard Safety Concerns in Keeping Cruise Ship in Miami Port," *Sun Sentinel* (May 27, 2001), <sun-sentinel.com>.

10 See Karl Ross, "Norway Calls off Seven-Day Journey: Company May Face Safety Sanctions," *Miami Herald* (May 30, 2001).

11 See "Europe Will Target Cruise Ships in Safety Campaign from 2003," *Lloyd's List* (July 16, 2001), <www.lloydslist.com>.

12 International Commission on Shipping, *Inquiry into Ship Safety: Ships, Slaves and Competition* (ICONS, 2000).

13 See "Europe Will Target Cruise Ships," *Lloyd's List* (July 16, 2001).

14 See "*Ocean Glory I* Plight 'Tip of the Iceberg' " *Lloyd's List* (July 9, 2001); and "Outrage over 'Death Trap' That Puts Passengers off Cruising," *Lloyd's List* (July 4, 2001); <www.lloydslist.com>.

15 See House of Representatives, *Effect of the Passenger Services Act on the Domestic Cruise Industry: Hearing before the Subcommittee on Coast Guard and Maritime Transportation of the Committee on Transportation and Infrastructure* (April 29, 1998), p. 171.

16 See David Olser, "Norwegian Dream Collision Report Blames 'Confused' Officer," *Lloyd's List* (May 22, 2000), p. 3; and "Recommendations of the Report," ibid.

17 See Joel Glass, "USCG Plea to IMO on Passenger Safety," *Lloyd's List* (June 10, 1992), p. 3.

18 See National Transportation Safety Board, *Marine Accident Report: Fire On Board the Panamanian Passenger Ship* Universe Explorer *in the Lynn Canal near Juneau, Alaska, July 27, 1996*, NTSB/MAR-98/02, 1998.

19 National Transportation Safety Board, *Marine Accident Brief: Fire Aboard the Passenger Ship* Vistafjord, *near Grand Bahama Island, Bahamas, April 6, 1997*, NTSB/MAR-98/01, 1998.

20 "Cruise Line Industry Security Issues," testimony of J. Michael Crye, (ICCL president) before the Senate Committee on Commerce, Science and Transportation, Subcommittee on Surface Transportation and Merchant Marine (October 2, 2001), <www.iccl.org/pressroom/testimony.pdf>.

21 Douglas Frantz, "On Cruise Ships, Silence Shrouds Crimes," *New York Times* (November 16, 1998), <www.nytimes.com>.

22 See Margaret Adams, "Rape Case Threatens Cruise Industry Image: Girl, 14, Says Crewman Assaulted Her," *Miami Herald*, Broward edition (February 5, 1990), p. A1.

23 Frantz, "On Cruise Ships, Silence Shrouds Crimes."

24 Ibid.

25 Jim Oliphant, "When the Fun Stops," *Miami Daily Business Review* (July 14, 1999), <http://www.floridabiz.com>.

26 See *Travel Weekly TW Crossroads Daily News* [e-letter] [June 28, 2001]. The need for proper caution is further reflected in an Associated Press story dated August 23, 2001, entitled "Pedophile Caught in Thailand Admits Porn Habit." The arrested man had been on the FBI's "Ten Most Wanted" list; he admitted that during his year as a fugitive he had played piano on a cruise ship between Hong Kong and the Mediterranean.

27 Douglas Frantz, "Cruise Line Reports 62 Alleged Sexual Assaults over

5 Years," *New York Times* (July 14, 1999). Also see Frantz, "Cruise Line Says It Underreported Allegations of Sexual Assault," *New York Times*, July 29, 1999; <www.nytimes.com>.

28 Wendy Doscher, "Carnival Settles with Jane Doe in Suit Alleging Sexual Assault," *Miami Daily Business Review* (December 2, 1999), <http://www.floridabiz.com>.

29 Susan Richards, "Pestered at Sea," *Los Angeles Times* (December 1, 1991), p. L22.

30 See Frantz, "On Cruise Ships, Silence Shrouds Crimes."

31 See Joel Glass, "Two Held for Cruise Death," *Lloyd's List* (March 4, 1993), p. 3.

32 See Frantz, "On Cruise Ships, Silence Shrouds Crimes"; and Tristram Korten, "Carnival? Try Criminal: What Happens when a Female Passenger Is Assaulted on a Cruise Ship? Not Much," *Miami New Times* (February 3-9, 2000), <www.miaminewtimes.com>.

33 Frantz, "On Cruise Ships, Silence Shrouds Crimes."

34 Nickie McWhirter, "Proposal Has Vacationers Cruising for a Bruising," *Detroit News* (August 29, 1995), p. F5.

35 Frantz, "On Cruise Ships, Silence Shrouds Crimes."

36 Korten, "Carnival? Try Criminal."

37 McWhirter, "Proposal Has Vacationers Cruising."

38 Frantz, "On Cruise Ships, Silence Shrouds Crimes."

39 Ibid.

40 Anne Kalosh, "Shipboard Confidential: Love, Sex, Death, and the Baron's Missing Trousers," *Los Angeles Times* (September 12, 1993), p. L1.

41 Frantz, "On Cruise Ships, Silence Shrouds Crimes."

42 Ibid.

43 See Korten, "Carnival? Try Criminal."

44 Tim Hornyak, "Healthy Cruising," *Medical Post* (July 6, 1999), p. 33.

45 See the Centers for Disease Control (CDC) Vessel Sanitation Program inspection for the *Seven Seas Navigator*, March 29, 2001, <www2.cdc.gov/nceh/vsp/VSP_InspRpt.asp?txtShip=SEVEN+SEAS+NAVIGATOR&txtDate=03/29/2001>.

46 See Dipesh Gadher, "Cruise Liners Face Tougher Hygiene Tests," *Sunday Times* (London) (May 6, 2001), <http://www.sundaytimes.co.uk>.

47 Several weeks after receiving a score of 91 on its heath inspection, Carnival Cruise Line's *Jubilee* had an outbreak of gastrointestinal disease that struck as many as 150 passengers. See Carla Rivera, "Ship Had Just Passed Inspection," *Los Angeles Times* (June 25, 1996), p. B1. Similarly, a no-sail order was issued in 1997 for Norwegian Cruise Line's Royal Odyssey following three successive outbreaks of illness caused by the Norwalk-like virus. The ship had received a passing score on its most recent inspection.

48 See Hans Hesselberg, "Food Safety," *Cruise Industry News Quarterly* (Fall 1995), p. 60.

49 N.A. Daniels et al., "Traveler's Diarrhea at Sea: Three Outbreaks of Waterborne Enterotoxigenic *Escherichia* coli on Cruise Ships," *Journal of Infectious Disease* 181, no. 4 (April 2000), pp. 1491-95.

50 See Centers for Disease Control, *Investigation Summary: Outbreak of Gastroenteritis Illness aboard the Cruise Ship* Disney Magic (June 2-5, 2000),<www.cdc.gov/nceh/vsp/outbreak/2000/DisneyMagicTRep ort.htm>; and CDC's *Investigation of Gastroenteritis aboard* Palm Beach Princess (May 18-19, 2000), <www.cdc.gov/nceh/vsp/outbreak/2000/PBPrincess.htm>.

51 See Centers for Disease Control, CDC's *Investigation of Gastroenteritis aboard* Spirit of Glacier Bay (May 28-June 1, 2000), <www.cdc.gov/nceh/vsp/outbreak/2000/spiritofglacierbay.htm>.

52 See Centers for Disease Control, *Investigation Summary: Outbreak of GI Illness aboard the Cruise Ship M/V* Nantucket Clipper (January 23-30, 2000 and February 6-13, 2000), *St. Thomas, US Virgin Islands*, <www.cdc.gov/nceh/vsp/outbreak/2000/Nclipper.htm>.

53 Ibid.

54 R.E. Pugh et al., "Onshore Catering Increases the Risk of Diarrhoeal Illness amongst Cruise Ship Passengers," *Communicable Disease Intelligence* 25, no. 1 (January 2001), pp. 15-17.

55 According to "Influenza in Travelers to Alaska, the Yukon Territory, and on West Coast Cruise Ships," *Canada Communicable Disease Report* 25, no. 16 (August 15, 1999), approximately 40,000 tourists and tourism workers experienced summertime outbreaks of influenza.

56 See "Influenza-A Outbreak on a Cruise Ship," *Canada Communicable Disease Report* 24, no. 2 (January 15, 1998).

57 Margaret Munro, "Influenza Takes a Cruise," *National Post* (August 7, 1999), p. B6.

58 T.J. Rowbotham, "Legionellosis Associated with Ships," *Journal of Communicable Disease and Public Health* 1, no. 3 (September 1998), pp. 146-51.

59 In his testimony before the House Committee on Merchant Marine and Fisheries, Subcommittee on Merchant Marine and Coast Guard and Navigation, on September 28, 1994, Richard J. Jackson (director of the National Center for Environmental Health) provides an overview of the Legionnaire's disease cases on the *Horizon*. He also discusses a food poisoning outbreak from shigellosis on Royal Caribbean Cruise Line's *Viking Serenade*. See Centers for Disease Control, <www.cdc.gov/nceh/programs/sanit/vsp/desc/vsptes.htm>.

60 "Cruise Ship Again Struck by Sickness," *New York Times* (July 24, 1995), <www.nytimes.com>.

61 Pastoris M. Castellani et al., "Legionnaire's Disease on a Cruise Ship Linked to the Water Supply System: Clinical and Public Health Implications," *Clinical Infectious Disease* 28, no. 1 (January 1999), pp. 33-38.

62 See "Rubella Outbreaks on Cruise Ships," *Canadian Medical Association Journal* 158, no. 4 (February 24, 1998), p. 516.

63 See "Addenda," *Washington Post* (January 9, 1998), p. A2. According to the article, health officials recommended that all crew members be vaccinated against measles, mumps, and rubella after an outbreak that sickened 22 crew members on two ships sailing between Florida and the Bahamas.

64 Kathleen Doheny, "Rubella Advisory Issued for Cruises," *Los Angeles Times* (January 18, 1998), p. L3.

65 "Clean Vents for Comfort and Safety," *Cruise Industry News Quarterly* (Winter 1998-99), pp. 40-42.

66 National Transportation Safety Board, *Marine Accident Report: Fire on board the Liberian Passenger Ship* Ecstasy, *Miami, Florida, July 20, 1998.*

67 "Health Scare in Wake of Pacific Cruise," *Seatrade Insider News* (January 25, 2002).

68 Douglas Frantz, "Getting Sick on the High Seas: A Question of Accountability," *New York Times* (October 31, 1999), <www.nytimes.com>.

69 See International Council of Cruise Lines, *ICCL Medical Facilities Guidelines Policy Statement* [updated January 1, 2002], <www.iccl.org/policies/medical2.htm>.

70 At the time the cost for an emergency airlift from a ship was between $20,000 and $50,000. See Kathleen Doheny, "Medical Costs Afloat," *Los Angeles Times* (February 11, 1996), p. L9.

71 Douglas Frantz, "Getting Sick on a Cruise May Mean Medical Care with Few Standards," *New York Times* (October 31, 1999), <www.nytimes.com>.

72 See Frantz, "Getting Sick on the High Seas" and "Getting Sick on a Cruise."

73 Frantz, "Getting Sick on a Cruise."

74 Ibid.

75 Ibid.

Chapter 4: "Save the Waves" — Sounds Good, But ...

1 Paul Queary, "Cruise Ship Dumping Sparks Interest," *Associated Press* (December 2, 1999).

2 Linda Nowlan and Ines Kwan, *Cruise Control: Regulating Cruise Ship Pollution on the Pacific Coast of Canada* (West Coast Environmental Law, 2001), p. 21.

3 In October 1992 the US government "told the International Maritime Organization's Marine Environmental Committee meeting that it had reported MARPOL violations to the appropriate flag states 111 times, but received responses in only about 10% of the cases." See "U.S. Cracks Down on Marine Pollution," *Lloyd's List* (April 17, 1993), p. 3.

4 See US General Accounting Office, *Marine Pollution: Progress Made to Reduce Marine Pollution by Cruise Ships, but Important Issues Remain,*

doc. no. GAO/RCED-00-48, February 2000.

5 Ocean Conservancy, *Cruise Control: A Report on How Cruise Ships Affect the Marine Environment* (Washington, DC: OC, May 2002), p. 40, <http://www.oceanconservancy.org/dynamic/aboutUs/publications/cruiseControl.pdf>

6 For details, see Joel Glass, "$250,000 Award for Reporting At-Sea Plastics Dumping," *Lloyd's List* (July 12, 1993), p. 1.

7 See William Booth, "Cruise Ship Owners Plead Guilty to Dumping Bilge Oil in Atlantic," *Washington Post* (June 4, 1994), p. A2.

8 James Vicini, "Focus — Royal Caribbean to Plead Guilty to Pollution," *Reuters* (July 21, 1999). Also see US Department of Justice press release, "Royal Caribbean to Pay Record $18 Million Criminal Fine for Dumping Oil and Hazardous Chemicals, Making False Statements," (July 21, 1999).

9 "'Sovereign of the Seas' Operator in Two Key Defensive Moves against Coast Guard Oil Dumping Charges," *Lloyd's List* (December 23, 1996), p. 3.

10 See Joel Glass, "Royal Caribbean Indicted after Alleged Oil Discharge off Puerto Rico," *Lloyd's List* (December 21, 1996), p. 1.

11 A detailed analysis (including diagrams) of the case involving the *Sovereign of the Seas* is provided in Gregg Fields, "Slick Justice," *Miami Herald* (September 26, 1999), <www.herald.com>. An analysis that includes the *Nordic Empress* and that looks at attempts to have the governments of Liberia and Norway intervene on Royal Caribbean Cruise Line's behalf is provided in Douglas Frantz, "Gaps in Sea Laws Shield Pollution by Cruise Lines," *New York Times* (January 3, 1999), <www.nytimes.com>.

12 See "After Apology and $9 Million Punishment, Royal Caribbean Dumps Again," *Washington Post* (October 25, 1998), p. E3.

13 Wendy Doscher, "Rough Seas for Cruise Line," *Miami Daily Business Review* (July 18, 2000), <www.floridabiz.com>.

14 See Sharon L. Crenson, "Cruise Ship Inquiry Expands," *Associated Press* (February 15, 2001).

15 For a straightforward description of Azipod technology, see Oivind Mathisen, "Increased Interest in Podded Drives," *Cruise Industry News Quarterly* (Spring 1999), pp. 112-16.

16 Ocean Conservancy, *Cruise Control.*

17 International Council of Cruise Lines press release, "Statement of the International Council of Cruise Lines (ICCL) Regarding Recent Environmental Settlement," (July 27, 1999), <www.iccl.org/press-room/press13.htm>.

18 Robinson Shaw, "Suit Filed over Cruise Line Pollution," *Environmental News Network* (July 6, 2000).

19 For an overview of international requirements, see Jack Polderman, *Environmental Protection for Cruise Ships: International and Local Requirements* (Lloyd's Register Americas, 2001).

20 See International Maritime Organization, *MARPOL 73/78 — Consolidated Edition, 1997: Articles, Protocols, Annexes, Unified Interpretations Of The International Convention For The Prevention Of Pollution From Ships, 1973, As Modified By The Protocol Of 1978 Relating Thereto*, 2nd ed. (IMO, 1997).

21 The National Research Council issued a 355-page study entitled *Clean Ships, Clean Ports, Clean Oceans* which called for strengthened enforcement of MARPOL's Annex V, particularly against foreign flag ships. Its calls had limited impact. For a summary of the report, see Joel Glass, "Research Council Report Targets Foreign-Flag Vessels," *Lloyd's List* (September 6, 1995), p. 1

22 See IMO, *MARPOL 73/78* (1997).

23 Kira Schmidt, *Cruising for Trouble: Stemming the Tide of Cruise Ship Pollution* (Bluewater Network, March 2000), <www.earthisland.org/bw/cruisereport.shtml>.

24 Ocean Conservancy, *Cruise Control*.

25 The industry's position was clearly and concisely articulated by Stein Kruse (senior vice-president of fleet operations, Holland America Line) in his presentation, "The Cruise Industry: Environmental Leadership," Seatrade Cruise Shipping Convention, Miami, FL, March 8, 2001.

26 For a more complete discussion, see Schmidt, *Cruising for Trouble*.

27 A comparison of American and Canadian laws is provided by Nowlan and Kwan in *Cruise Control*.

28 Schmidt, *Cruising for Trouble*.

29 See H.R. 5666, *Making Miscellaneous Appropriations for the Fiscal Year Ending September 30, 2001, and for Other Purposes* (Government Printing Office, 2000).

30 There is a question of how much plastic is incinerated at sea by cruise ships. The by-products left in the ash can be harmful to sea life and the environment.

31 It is worth noting that Alaska's regulations are tighter than federal limits, at 10 parts per million, on the release of aromatic hydrocarbons.

32 Frantz, "Gaps in Sea Laws Shield Pollution."

33 See Doug O'Harra, "Whales in Sound Imperiled: Orcas Poisons May Be Driving Unique Family to Extinction," *Anchorage Daily News* (July 22, 2001), <www.adn.com>.

34 For a more detailed discussion of the effects of ocean pollution, see Nowlan and Kwan, *Cruise Control*.

35 Charlie Anderson, "Are We Killing Our Whales?", *Vancouver Province* (June 24, 2001), <www.vancouverprovince.com>.

36 See O'Harra, "Whales in Sound Imperiled."

37 As stated by the judge, because the fine was paid promptly, he suspended half of the $6-million penalty. The original fine of $6.5 million was for dumping toxic chemicals and oil-contaminated water into Alaska's waters. The case had initially been filed in August 1999; Royal Caribbean Cruise Line paid the fines in January 2000.

38 See Seth Zuckerman, "Come Again, But Leave Your Tour at Home," *Tidepool Archives* (October 6, 1999), <www.tidepool.org>.

39 Nowlan and Kwan, *Cruise Control*, p. 16.

40 Holland America Line retaliated against Juneau's new head tax with an announcement that it would withdraw much of its support to local charities. Al Parrish (a company vice-president) reportedly said, "If the community doesn't really want us there, if that's really truly what they're telling us, then we need to reassess what we're doing." See Yereth Rosen, "Alaska Officials Plan Crackdown on Cruise Ships," *Reuters* (February 22, 2000).

41 "Lines May Fight Legality of Juneau Passenger Levy," *Lloyd's List* (October 8, 1999), p. 5.

42 In 2000 Senator Rick Halford, a conservative Republican from Anchorage, sponsored the first bill in the state Senate to impose a $50-per-person head tax. The legislation was introduced in the state House by liberal Democrat Beth Kerttula from Juneau. The bill passed the Senate, but industry lobbying of committee chairpersons effectively prevented it from being heard by the House. See John McLaughlin, "The *Sun Princess* Has Helped Turn Alaska into a Popular Destination, But Now Faces a Swinging Tax from the State Senate," *Lloyd's List* (April 26, 2000), p. 1; and Paul Queary, "Alaskan Senate OKs Cruise Ship Tax," *Associated Press* (April 21, 2000).

43 "Knowles Introduces Head Tax to Alaska Lawmakers," *Seatrade Insider News* (February 12, 2002).

44 See Alaska Office of the Governor press release #00252, "Knowles Steps up Pressure on Congress for Action on Cruise Ship Discharges," (October 6, 2000), <www.gov.state.ak.us/press/00252.html>.

45 A number of explanations were explored for finding fecal coliform in graywater — including the possibility that open drains in the galley had been used by some crew members in place of the toilet — but no consensus was reached. Fecal coliform counts in graywater were reported to be higher than 20 million/ml; the allowable limit is 200/ml. See Alaska Governor press release, "Knowles Steps up Pressure."

46 See Bill McAllister, "A Big Violation on Wastewater: Some Ship Readings 100,000 Times Allowed Amount," *Juneau Empire* (August 27, 2000), <www.juneauempire.com>.

47 See Bill McAllister, "Cruise Initiative Brought about Federal, State Laws," *Juneau Empire*, November 18, 2001, <www.juneauempire.com>.

48 In particular, federal legislation passed in December 2000 provides that "the geometric mean of the samples from discharge during any 30-day period does not exceed 20 fecal coliform/100 ml and not more than 10 percent of the samples exceed 40 fecal coliform/100 ml." See H.R. 5666, Section 1404 (C.3).

49 See Alaska Cruise Ship Initiative, *Commercial Passenger Vessel Environmental Compliance Program: 2001 Legislative Summary*, <www.state.ak.us/dec/press/cruise/legsummary2001.htm>.

50 See Yereth Rosen, "Alaskans See Drawbacks to Booming Cruise Business," *Reuters*, (June 29, 2001).

51 Bill McAllister, "Celebrity Illegally Dumping in Port," *Juneau Empire* (June 5, 2001), <www.juneauempire.com>.

52 Kathy Dye, "Ship Pumps Laundry Water into City Harbor," *Juneau Empire* (June 19, 2001), <www.juneauempire.com>.

53 The full report *Interim Cruise Ship Sampling Data Summary* is available on-line at <www.state.ak.us/dec/press/cruise/pdfs/interim-summ090601.pdf>.

54 See "Babbitt OKs Rise in Glacier Bay Traffic," *Los Angeles Times* (December 22, 1994), p. A25.

55 See Tom Kenworthy, "Babbit Orders Park Service to Endorse Increase of Cruise Ships in Glacier Bay," *Washington Post* (December 21, 1994), p. A4. Interestingly, Bruce Babbitt was Secretary of the Interior at the time. His former law firm represents Holland America Line, which has the largest number of permits to Glacier Bay; see Tom Kenworthy, "Tour Operator Was Client of Babbitt's Ex-Law Firm," *Washington Post* (January 24, 1995), p. A9.

56 See Paula Dobbyn, "Bill Would Aid Glacier Bay Ships," *Anchorage Daily News* (July 13, 2001), <www.adn.com>.

57 Yereth Rosen, "Blow to Head Kills Alaska Humpback Whale," *Reuters*, (July 25, 2001).

58 "Cruise Lines Give $75,000 to GOP After Judge Lifts Donations Cap," *Associated Press* (July 23, 2001). It is also worth noting that in 1998 Alaska congressman Don Young, through his role as chairperson of the House Committee on Resources, preserved foreign cruise lines' monopoly on entry permits to Glacier Bay National Park until 2009. Congressman Young received $45,000 in contributions from cruise industry employees in recent years; one of his former staff members now works as the chief lobbyist for Holland America Line, which holds the largest number of permits to Glacier Bay. See Douglas Frantz, "Cruise Lines Profit from Friends in Congress," *New York Times* (February 19, 1999), <www.nytimes.com>.

59 Cruise lines have for many years played ports against each other as a way of resisting increased port charges or other issues. This was identified by the Caribbean Hotel Association as a major concern as early as 1991. See David Renwick, "Cruise Lines 'Harm' Caribbean," *Lloyd's List* (March 12, 1991), p. 2. In 1992, when the Organization of Eastern Caribbean States (OECS) increased head taxes, cruise lines threatened to boycott countries that levy rates they consider unreasonable. See "Caribbean 'Head Tax' Row Looms," *Lloyd's List* (February 19, 1992), p. 3.

60 See David Renwick, "Bahamian Ports Face Boycott Threat," *Lloyd's List* (June 15, 1992), p. 3.

61 "Lines Resist Caribbean Tax," *Lloyd's List* (March 31, 1994), p. 18.

62 "Jamaica and Cruise Lines Reach Tax Compromise," *Miami Herald* (August 27, 1993), <www.herald.com>.

63 Mark Fineman, "Tax on Passengers is a Lot of Garbage, Cruise Lines Say," *Los Angeles Times* (March 20, 1998), p. A5.

64 Ibid.

65 David Renwick, "Carnival Boycotts Grenada in Levy Row," *Lloyd's List* (November 15, 1999), p. 5.

66 See "Tougher Approach to Waste Disposal," *Lloyd's List* (March 11, 1992), p. 2.

67 See "Fine Highlights Caribbean Waste Problem," *Lloyd's List* (April 9, 1993), p. 3.

68 "Caribbean Ports 'Not Enforcing' Green Laws," *Lloyd's List* (June 24, 1992), p. 3.

69 Industry insiders rarely address this issue. For one viewpoint, see Anre Baekkelund, "Solving the People Pollution Problem," *Seatrade Cruise Review* (December 1999), p. 61.

Chapter 5: Below the Passenger Deck

1 International Transport Workers' Federation, "The Dark Side of the Cruise Industry," *Seafarers' Bulletin* 14 (2000), p. 17.

2 International Commission on Shipping, *Inquiry into Ship Safety: Ships, Slaves and Competition* (ICONS, 2000), p. 59.

3 Heinz Niedermaier, "The Future of F&B," *Cruise Industry News Quarterly* (Summer 1999), p. 44.

4 "Crew Count Set to Double," *Lloyd's List* (June 9, 2001), <www.lloydslist.com>.

5 ICONS, *Inquiry into Ship Safety*.

6 Christopher Reynolds and Dan Weikel, "For Cruise Workers, Voyages Are No Vacations," *Los Angeles Times* (May 30, 2000), p. T5.

7 Paul K. Chapman, *Trouble on Board: The Plight of International Seafarers* (ILR Press, 1992), p. 56.

8 Kirk Nielsen, "The Perfect Scam: For the Workers Life Is No Carnival, Believe It or Not," *Miami New Times* (February 3-9, 2000), <www.miaminewtimes.com>.

9 Chapman, *Trouble on Board*, p. 67.

10 Anne Kalosh, "Shipboard Confidential: Love, Sex, Death, and the Barron's Missing Trousers," *Los Angeles Times* (September 12, 1993), p. L1.

11 See "Cruise Line Settles Suit by Ex-Worker Citing Rape," *New York Times* (December 5, 1999), p. 40.

12 "Former Employee Claims Luxury Liner Allowed Sexually Charged Working Environment," *SF Gate News* (December 7, 1998).

13 Ibid.

14 ICONS, *Inquiry into Ship Safety*, p. 60.

15 Filipino workers typically pay $1,500 to join a cruise ship. See ITF,"The Dark Side of the Cruise Industry."

16 Reynolds and Weikel, "For Cruise Workers, Voyages Are No

Vacations." In many cases, the cruise line advances the cost of airfare and deducts the cost from employees' paychecks. See Kevin Moran, "Lost at Sea: Cruise Workers Must Endure Long Hours for Others' Leisure," *Houston Chronicle* (September 29, 1996), p. 28.

17 Chapman, *Trouble on Board,* p. 32.

18 Joshua Harris Prager, "For Cruise Workers, Life Is No 'Love Boat'," *Wall Street Journal* (July 3, 1997), p. B1.

19 Nielsen, "The Perfect Scam."

20 One reporter suggests that the threat of returning to an economic disaster area back home keeps workers on Carnival's payroll, earning $550 a month — a wage far below the poverty level in the United States. The company's response is along the lines of: "If you don't like the salary, you can go." As one worker comments, "It's like blackmail." See Nielsen, "The Perfect Scam."

21 See, for example, H.R. 03-818, *Coverage of Certain Federal Labor Laws to Foreign Documented Vessels* (Government Printing Office, 1994), p. 3; and Joel Glass, "House Subcommittee Reviews Bogey of Maritime Labour Law," *Lloyd's List* (October 10, 1992), p. 4.

22 Nielsen, "The Perfect Scam."

23 In Paul Courtice, "Have MD, Will Travel" (*Medical Post,* October 19, 1999, p. 27), the author suggests that "when the captain withholds the stabilizers, he is rewarded by saving fuel, food, and additionally makes a percentage on resulting pharmaceutical sales." The food savings and increased pharmaceutical sales are the result of a greater incidence of seasickness due to the stabilizers not being used. The stabilizers' function is to help keep the ship stable (by reducing side-to-side movement) but the ship burns more fuel when they are in use.

24 A ship's physician reportedly receives 20 percent of medical fees collected; the nurse receives 10 percent. See Courtice, "Have MD, Will Travel."

25 Joel Glass, "ICCL Gives Ultimatum to House of Representatives Sub-Committee on Relocation of Foreign-Flag Vessels," *Lloyd's List* (May 15, 1993), p. 3. For further detail, see US Congress, *Hearing on H.R. 1517, Foreign Flag Ships: Hearing before the Subcommittee on Labor Standards, Occupational Health, and Safety of the Committee on Education and Labor, House of Representatives,* 103rd Cong., 1st sess., May 13, 1993 (Government Printing Office, 1993), Y 4.ED 8/1:103-09.

26 International Transport Workers' Federation, *Big Red Bombshell* (ITF, February 2001), p. 6.

27 See, for example, Chapman, *Trouble on Board.*

28 See ITF, *Big Red Bombshell,* p. 6.

29 See International Transport Workers' Federation, *Flags of Convenience,* (ITF, 1999).

30 ICONS, *Inquiry into Ship Safety,* pp. 59-60.

31 See Carnival Corporation's annual reports for 1999 and 2000,

<www.carnivalcorp.com>.

32 Felix Chan, "Panama Slammed for Being Worst Flag State in the World," *InforMARE*, February 25, 1999, <www.infomare.it/news/review/1999/st0734.asp>.

33 See International Transport Workers' Federation, <www.itf.org.uk/seafarers/cruise_ships/message_to_employees.htm>.

34 See Jim Morris, "'Flags of Convenience' Give Owners a Paper Refuge," *Houston Chronicle*, August 21, 1996, <www.chron.com/content/interactive/special/maritime/96/08/22/part5.html>

Chapter 6: Everything Would Run Fine ... But Passengers Keep Getting in the Way

1   The short life of a website critical of the QE 2 and Cunard Line, which disappeared from the Internet less than two weeks after it began, was a topic of discussion on the "rec.travel.cruises" Usenet newsgroup between January 9 and January 12, 2000. The *QE 2* website had been put up after an unsatisfactory experience on a millennium cruise; the person behind it was seeking others to join in a group appeal for compensation from Cunard. Less than a week after the *QE 2* website was called to the attention of the Usenet discussion group, it was removed. A message posted on the discussion group by the website's owner stated that Cunard had settled with him.

2   Cynthia Corzo, "When Cruises Go Awry, You're at Mercy of Line," *Miami Herald* (February 7, 1999), <www.herald.com>.

3   See "Passengers Attack Mistral Compensation," *Lloyd's List* (March 5, 2001), <www.lloydslist.com>.

4   "Bush Reporters Offered Free Cruise," *Associated Press* (July 24, 2001).

5   "Royal Caribbean Cruise Line Appears to Have Come Up with a Novel Way of Dealing with Dirty Laundry," *Lloyd's List* (May 19, 1997), p. 5.

6   "Mathews Slugs It Out with Carnival," *Lloyd's List* (January 22, 1998), p. 5.

7   "Suit against Miami-Based Cruise Line Refiled There," *Houston Chronicle* (February 3, 1998), <www.chron.com>.

8   "Grandfather's Ashes Lost in Cruise Ship Grounding," *Reuters*, (February 10, 1999).

9   Ronald K. Fitten, "Seattle-Based Cruise Line Accused in Drowning," *Seattle Times* (August 9, 1999), <www.seattletimes.com>.

10 Ibid.

11 Brian Major, "Court Will Hear Class Action Suit against NCL," *Travel Weekly TW Crossroads Daily News* [e-letter] (March 8, 2001).

12 Leith L. Alexander, "Shoved Off the Love Boat," *Washington Post* (May 19, 2001), p. E1.

13 Ibid.

Chapter 7: What Can Be Done?

1   International Commission on Shipping, *Inquiry into Ship Safety: Ships, Slaves and Competition* (ICONS, 2000), pp. 177-78.

2   Ibid., p. 178.

3   Kevin Moran, "Lost at Sea: Cruise Workers Endure Long Hours for Others' Leisure," *Houston Chronicle* (September 29, 1996), p. 28.

4   "Yakatut Bills Ships for Visits to Bay," *Anchorage Daily News* (January 6, 2002), <www.adn.com>.

Appendix A

1   The cause was a hot water kettle that set a crew cabin on fire. The NTSB found that officers ignored their own shipboard firefighting plan. As a result, the fire spread beyond the cabin, smoke reached upper decks, and contact with the Coast Guard was not made for nearly an hour. See Joling, Dan. "NTSB Report Faults Crew in Ship Fire" *Associated Press Wire Service* (September 29, 2001).

2   See Immen, Wallace. "Dream Cruise a Nightmare After Ship's Power Fails," *Globe and Mail* (February 8, 2000), p. A-5.

INDEX

ABOUT THE AUTHOR

Ross Klein was introduced to cruising when as a youngster his parents took him on cruises to Hawaii (1963) and Alaska (1968). He took his first cruise as an adult in 1974 on the Mikhail Lermontov — the first year a Russian ship embarked from a US port. In 1992, he returned to cruising and in the next 9 years took 30 cruises comprising approximately 300 days. With each cruise he gained a deeper understanding of the cruise industry and its well-concealed underside.

Ross's education is in sociology and social work. He worked as a social group worker following completion of his Masters degree in social work in 1974. In 1981 he completed his PhD in sociology with a focus on nonviolent alternatives to war. He is presently on the faculty of the School of Social Work, Memorial University of Newfoundland.

Ross lives with his partner in St. John's, Newfoundland. He is a board member of Family Service Canada and an advocate for change in the cruise ship industry. He no longer takes cruises, preferring land-based vacations instead — at least until the cruise industry cleans up its act.

Ross is on-line at:
www.cruisejunkie.com

If you have enjoyed *Cruise Ship Blues*, you might enjoy other

BOOKS TO BUILD A NEW SOCIETY

Our books provide positive solutions for people who want
to make a difference. We specialize in:

• Conscientious Commerce • Progressive Leadership •
• Sustainable Living • Ecological Design and Planning •
• Natural Building & Appropriate Technology • New Forestry •
• Educational and Parenting Resources • Environment and Justice •
• Resistance and Community • Nonviolence

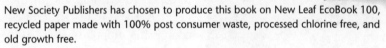

New Society Publishers

ENVIRONMENTAL BENEFITS STATEMENT

New Society Publishers has chosen to produce this book on New Leaf EcoBook 100,
recycled paper made with 100% post consumer waste, processed chlorine free, and
old growth free.

For every 5,000 books printed, New Society saves the following resources:[1]

23	Trees
2,120	Pounds of Solid Waste
2,332	Gallons of Water
3,042	Kilowatt Hours of Electricity
3,853	Pounds of Greenhouse Gases
17	Pounds of HAPs, VOCs, and AOX Combined
6	Cubic Yards of Landfill Space

[1]Environmental benefits are calculated based on research done by the Environmental Defense Fund and
other members of the Paper Task Force who study the environmental impacts of the paper industry.

For more information on this environmental benefits statement, or to inquire about environmentally
friendly papers, please contact New Leaf Paper – info@newleafpaper.com Tel: 888 • 989 • 5323.

For a full list of NSP's titles, please call **1-800-567-6772** *or check out our web site at:*

www.newsociety.com

NEW SOCIETY PUBLISHERS